The Swimmer

and other stories of life

Edited by
Mark Worthing, Pete Court & James Cooper

ISBN 978-0-6488957-3-2

Compilation copyright © Mark Worthing, Pete Court and James Cooper 2020
Copyright of individual chapters remains with the author of those chapters.

All rights reserved. Other than for the purposes and subject to the conditions prescribed under the Copyright Act, no part of this publication may be reproduced, stored in a retrieval system, or transmitted in any form or by any means, electronic, mechanical, photocopying, recording or otherwise, without the prior permission of the publisher.

Cataloguing-in-Publication entry is available from the National Library of Australia http:/catalogue.nla.gov.au/.

This edition first published in 2020

Cover art and typesetting by Ben Morton

Published in Australia by Immortalise via Ingram Spark
www.immortalise.com.au

cover image source ID 125335038 © Pp1 | Dreamstime.com

Sponsors

We wish to thank the following organisations for their sponsorship of the Stories of Life creative writing competition and publishing venture:

 **Tabor College of Higher Education** — sponsor of the 2020 Stories of Life Open Award for stories up to 1500 words.

 **Eternity Matters** — sponsor of the 2020 Stories of Life Short Award for stories up to 500 words.

 **Immortalise** — sponsor of the 2020 Stories of Life Youth Award for stories up to 1000 words by writers 17 and under.

Thanks also to **1079 Life** for their help with promotion and support for Stories of Life.

Introduction

The Swimmer, and other stories of life is the fifth time a collection of stories has been gathered from you, or people like you, and presented in one place. Once again, this year, the stories cover a vast amount of ground. There are very personal stories of life and death, big stories of small events and the small moments that make all lives special. The authors range in age from the very young to the very... experienced... and the variety of settings and styles continues to amaze. This year continues a trend toward ever more diversity in the story tellers. We've had tales from Africa and many corners of Asia as well as from Europe, across Australia and from our own back yard. It is an exciting trend we hope will continue into the future because, through all of these stories, the truth of a personal and loving God shines. And his story is global and deeply personal. If you have not shared *your* story of personal faith and testimony, your *Story of Life*, no matter how big or small it may be, you will find a home for it here. For now, enjoy this year's collection and know you are part of it too.

Pete Court
on behalf of the 2020 editorial team

Special thanks for the 2020 *Stories of Life* goes to our generous and wonderful competition judges.

Corrin Townsend judged the *Immortalise Young Stories of Life* category. For thirty-five years she has been sharing her love of reading and writing with the students of Concordia College, Cornerstone College and now Unity College in Murray Bridge.

David Rawlings judged the *Eternity Matters Short Stories of Life* category. David is an award-winning South Australian author who writes modern-day parables, stories that lift the lid on life and allow God to whisper to us all. His debut novel, *The Baggage Handler,* won the 2019 Christy Award for Best First Novel. His second novel, *The Camera Never Lies*, is now available and *Where the Road Bends*, based in finding yourself while lost in outback Australia, arrives soon.

Nola Passmore judged the *Tabor Open Stories of Life* category. Nola and her husband, Tim, run a freelance writing and editing business called *The Write Flourish*. She brings a wealth of experience as a university academic, with qualifications in psychology, creative writing, and Christian ministry. Nola has had more than 150 short pieces published, including short fiction, true stories, poetry, devotions, inspirational pieces, magazine articles, and academic papers. Her debut novel *Scattered* is currently in production

Contents

Introduction...iv

The Swimmer..1
    Gaynor Faulkner

The Ring...3
    Jo-Anne Berthelsen

The Refugee..8
    Charles Yuen

A Small Giveaway..12
    Jenine Altmann

The Anthill..14
    Diana Davison

Suicide is not a Book in the Fiction Section..16
    Isabel Barton

Graves to Gardens..19
    Martina Kontos

Slightly Awkward...23
    Esther Cremona

The Perfect Song..28
    Kaitlin Turland

The Crucible...30
    Judith Noyes

An Unexpected Adventure...34
    Heather Gray

An Experience that Changed Me...38
    Ellisa Thong

A Timeless Symphony...40
    Stephanie Taylor

Saved by Subtitles..42
    Boo Hooi Khoo

Palm Trees, Sand Dunes and Beach Umbrellas......................................44
    Diana Davison

In the Green..47
   Liz Donald

On the Way to Somewhere..51
   Margot Ogilvie

The Holiday 56
   Nesta Hatendi

My Two Mothers..60
   Donna Meehan

Unexpected Grace..64
   Kylie Gardiner

The Kodak Moment..68
   Stephanie Taylor

Sprinkled with Surprises..72
   Liisa Grace-Baun

Sign Language..77
   Julia Archer

An Imperfect Mum...81
   Karen Curran

Snakes, Ladders and Green Carpets...83
   Anusha Atukorala

His Eye is on the Budgie..88
   Lesley Beth Manuel

A Letter to You..90
   Beverly Sweeney

God's Love in the Home 92
   Colleen Russell

That Wonderful Peace..94
   Jeanette Grant-Thomson

The Way to Remember..96
   Jennie Del Mastro

With You..98
   Lisa Birch

In God's Garden...102
   Heather Gray

Only a Male 104
    R.J. Rodda

Pterodactyl 106
    Grant Lock

Our Story during the Pandemic 108
    Cris Yu

Twenty Square Centimetres of Power 110
    Margot Ogilvie

Peacock 112
    Juni Desireé Hoel

Where is God in my COVID-19 World? 114
    John Duthie

Jerusalem, in Egypt 116
    Elizabeth Tobal

That Question 118
    Anna Kosmanovski

Promised Rescue 120
    Emma Taylor

A Leap of Faith 122
    M. J. Saladine

Selective listening 125
    Anan Mclean

Lonely No More 129
    Isaac Wong

The Fighter 131
    Bastien Lee

He Answered 134
    Sheann Tung

Surviving the Lockdown 136
    Amelia Shee

Light Expels Darkness 138
    Magda Alef

An Angel in Heaven Now 143
    Hazel Barker

My Piano Solo 148
    Caleb Cheah

Invitation to Dance 151
    Rhonda Pooley

My Asthma Story 155
    Moses Yong

Misunderstood 157
    Val Russell

Andy 161
    Craig Chapman

Another Happy Memoir 163
    Baxter Gierus-Heintze

Suitcases 166
    Elizabeth Turland

The Swimmer

Gaynor Faulkner

One day last summer I went to the beach much earlier than usual. A scorching hot day had been forecast and I wanted to miss the midday heat. After a refreshing swim in the sea, I found a patch of shade at the top of the beach near some steps and reclined languidly on my towel.

I was nearly asleep when I heard a loud panting sound emanating from behind me. It sounded like an animal in pain. I swivelled around to see a young man and a feeble, elderly woman laboriously making their way down the stairs. The old lady's cautious steps were small and so precarious that I feared she'd topple down.

The friend accompanying her didn't seem at all perturbed by the old woman's frailty. He held her firmly and shuffled slowly alongside her with patience and precision — despite that, it seemed to take forever. I surmised he was her carer.

Once at the bottom of the steps, the man proceeded to lead the woman towards the sea. The old lady hooked her arm through his, clinging to his strength with all her life. Her steps were painstaking and laboured — so quivery and uncertain that it seemed like she might be carried away in the summer breeze.

I felt a pang in my chest as I watched her. A sadness. As the pair shuffled past me, I could see that the lady was ancient — maybe over a hundred years old. The skin on her face was translucent and papery, like a much-read family bible. Her white legs, thin and rickety, had a network of blue veins as intricate as lace.

By the time the pair made it to the water, I was back in myself. The old lady looked diminutive in the sea, despite support from her friend. When they reached deeper water, her companion gently let her go and swam away. My heart skipped a beat. But the old lady just serenely lay her head on the water. Clouds of white hair cascaded around her head like a halo.

And then she was off! She glided against the tide with long, powerful strokes. And adroitly sliced through the waves in wide circles. I couldn't believe the change in her — it was as if she were a snake shedding its skin. Now, she was a young Olympian swimmer. Powerful and fearless. Her strokes were strong and steady. Effortless. She passed by a myriad of other swimmers with ease. I saw her face as she swam past me — it radiated youthful joy.

The old lady swam to her companion then and it was apparently time to go because he guided her to the water's edge. It shocked me to see her helpless again — shaky and dependent once more, as she made the laborious journey back up the beach.

That transformation. That change, from very old to brand new — I think about it sometimes. To me, it felt like a glimpse of heaven.

The Ring
Jo-Anne Berthelsen

It's gone.

She gazes down at her hand in horror. Perhaps she's dreaming. Perhaps it's only one of those scary nightmares she sometimes has. But she can feel the warm sun on her arms and hear the seagulls screeching further down the beach. And there are her two younger brothers, playing nearby in the sand dunes.

She looks at her hand again. It's true. Her precious gold ring has disappeared.

She stands up, trying not to disturb the sand nearby — she doesn't want to bury the ring by accident. She checks all around her beautiful sandcastle. It took ages to build it and decorate all the walls with the shells she gathered earlier in her bucket. The bucket! Perhaps that's where her ring is.

With trembling fingers, she scrabbles around in the few shells left in it, but to no avail.

She brushes her dress down and looks in her pocket. Perhaps she's forgotten putting the ring there for safe keeping. After all, she waited so long for it and knows how valuable it is.

'If that's what you want, Ruth,' her father had told her, 'it will have to be a combined birthday and Christmas present. Let's see — it's October now. That's not long to wait.'

It had seemed like forever to her. All the popular girls at school had one, and she wanted to be the same as they were, with all her heart. She was different enough — the only one in her class whose mother had died — and she'd looked forward so much to showing off the ring when school started again. True, hers didn't have a red ruby in the corner like her best friend's did, or even a tiny diamond. But it had a pretty, gold pattern on each side, and there, right in the middle, were her initials: R.S.

When she'd first opened her present, she thought the S was a T.

'No, Ruth,' her father had reassured her. 'It's a fancy, old-fashioned S that the old man in the shop likes to use when he engraves things.'

She'd swallowed hard, trying to hide her disappointment. It was still a lovely ring, after all. With pride, she twirled her hand around until the ring flew off and landed on the floor.

'Hmm, I can see it's a bit big,' her father said. 'Still, you'll soon grow into it. Anyway, it'd cost too much to have it made smaller. I'll wind some cotton around it so it stays on better.'

That had disappointed her a little, too. But she knew there was no money to spare, so it was better to be grateful for what she had received. And she loved it anyway.

Only now her precious ring is gone. There's nothing but sand in her pocket.

Her mind's in a whirl. She knew it was unwise to wear any sort of jewellery down to the beach, but it's too late to think about that now. Her ring has to be somewhere nearby — she'd been in the same spot the whole morning, except when she went looking for shells. She checks the surrounding sand again, turning over each handful with care. Nothing. All she can do now is knock down her beautiful sandcastle and search through every part of it.

She sets to it with a heavy heart and, as she rakes through the towers and then the walls, her heart sinks even further. All that time and effort wasted. And, on top of that, still no sign of the ring.

At last, she heads up to the sand dunes where her brothers were playing.

'What's the matter?' John asks her straight away.

'I've lost my ring,' she quavers, trying to hold back her sobs.

She can tell they feel sorry for her, as they abandon their game and follow her down to the beach. They do their best to help look for her ring, but soon decide it's hopeless and give up.

Eventually, she sits back on her heels and looks around. She seems to have been searching for hours. Now the tide's coming in

The Ring

— little by little, the waves are creeping closer to her sandcastle, filling the ditch she dug around its walls. Soon anything that remains of her day's work will be washed away. Soon it will all disappear, just like her precious ring.

There's nothing for it. She will have to go back to the tent and tell her father.

'What's the matter, Ruth?' he asks, as soon as he sees her.

'My ring!' she sobs, tears dripping off her chin. 'I've lost my ring! I looked all around where I was on the beach — I couldn't find it anywhere!'

It's good to feel her father's arms around her, as he holds her close and tries to comfort her. But she can hear the resigned note in his voice, and her heart sinks again.

'Oh dear! Well, it's too late now to go down to the beach again. I'll help you look tomorrow. But you know I can't afford to buy you another one, so let's ask God to help us find it.'

It's almost impossible to eat dinner that night — every mouthful tastes like sand. And afterwards, when her father reads the Bible to them as he always does, and leads the family in prayer it's hard to concentrate. Even when they pray about the ring, she can only half join in — she's so sure she'll never see it again. After all, she looked everywhere for it.

Later, when her brothers play games before heading for bed, she doesn't have the heart to join them. Instead, she lies on her stretcher, rubbing the spot on her finger where her ring should be, trying not to cry.

The next morning she wakes when her father gives her shoulder a gentle shake.

'Come on, sleepyhead — it's time for breakfast!'

She dresses and begins eating, still only half awake. Then, in a rush, she remembers her ring. She pushes her plate aside — she doesn't feel like any more breakfast.

'I have to look for my ring straight away, Dad,' she says, trying to keep her voice steady.

'Well... okay then. I'll come and help as soon as I can — there are a few other things I need to do first. I think it might be hard to find your ring in all that sand, Ruth. But let's pray about it again before you go.'

She heads straight to the spot where she built her sandcastle, but just as she had expected, the tide has washed most of it away. All that remains are two small mounds of sand and a few shells.

She plops down and stares around her. Her ring could be anywhere — even far out in the ocean by now. In that case, finding her ring will perhaps be too hard even for God. Or perhaps God doesn't care at all about little things like rings.

She stays where she is, hoping her father will soon come. He'll do his best to find it, she knows.

The sand around her is dry now, and as she waits she idly scoops up a pile with both hands and lets it sift slowly through her fingers, over and over. It's something to do — and it feels quite soothing. Suddenly, she stops...

What's that? She's quite sure she saw something glinting in the sand as it fell. Could it be?

No, surely not — that's impossible.

Yes... yes! She's found it!

With shaking hands, she picks up her ring and wipes the sand off it. How can this be? She'd looked in that exact spot the day before and the ring had been nowhere in sight. It's as if it sat there all night, determined to wait for her to come back and find it.

She stands up and, with a little dance of joy, pushes her ring back on her finger. She gazes down at it for a moment, admiring the way it gleams in the sun. It looks even more beautiful than before, with her initials on it — her own special ring that she almost lost forever.

The Ring

As she runs to tell her father and brothers, her heart soars like the seagulls flying above her in the blue sky. God cared enough to make sure she found her ring again. God did something that seemed impossible — just for her.

The Refugee
Charles Yuen

The 'Butterfly Effect' that suggests the flapping wings of a butterfly in the Amazon can lead to a tornado in Texas, applies equally to human activities. One random act of kindness can lead to multiple unforeseeable outcomes. That was what I experienced with Raj and his wife, Parmita.

They came to me twelve years ago for legal advice when I was practicing as a migration lawyer in the Northern Territory. Raj and Parmita had recently arrived from India on visitor visas, apparently escaping from a horrendous situation back home. Born into a Hindu family, Raj and his wife had recently converted to Christianity, something frowned upon by their community. At the same time, he had upset some local criminal elements in the course of his business by refusing to cooperate with the local thugs seeking to use his business as a front for drug deals. They had begun to threaten him and his family and were using the thugs' connections with local authorities and police to lay false charges against him. His mother and brother had been attacked in order to put pressure on him to comply with their demands. The thugs had also incited the local community to turn on him for converting to Christianity. This was potentially life threatening.

Raj wanted to apply for a protection visa to allow himself and his wife to gain asylum in Australia. My experience dealing with such cases told me that even if his story could be proved, his chances of success were low because India is a big country and the Immigration Department would argue that he could move safely to another part of India to avoid the persecution. However, Raj insisted that I represent him despite the poor prospects of success. I had successfully helped a few refugee and other detention cases on a pro-bono basis, previously, but did not really have time to handle non-detention cases. I was a sole practitioner, and from a business perspective asylum cases were complicated, and clients were often highly emotional and overly demanding. Moreover, it was difficult to charge my usual fee because such clients were normally not permitted to work, and I knew Raj would soon run out of money. Unfortunately, the protection visa is often abused by those desperate to stay in the country, and this is often reflected in the low success rate of such applications. Yet there was something in Raj's demeanor telling me that he was genuine, and that I was his only hope. So, rather reluctantly, I accepted his case and agreed to charge quite a reduced service fee for the application.

As expected, the application was refused by the immigration department in the first instance and Raj was obliged to appeal to the Migration Review Tribunal for a review of the refusal. Because he was not in migration detention, Raj's case was given a low priority and so he could expect a long wait for a hearing before the MRT. In fact, the wait dragged out for six years. Normally, a person whose visa application is refused would be allowed to work on a bridging visa while waiting for their appeal. In the case of protection visa applicants, however, the right to work is not normally granted unless the applicant can prove financial hardship — something that is very subjective in the eyes of the immigration department. This was a risk Raj was well aware of when he chose to apply for asylum.

About a year after lodging the MRT review, Raj came to my office one day to ask me how he could get permission to work. In tears, he described how over the past year he and his wife had been living off the charity of friends they had met through the local Indian Christian community, which was quite small. He desperately needed to work. My heart was filled with compassion even though in my profession I frequently encountered clients going through very difficult times. I maintained my calm, professional exterior and advised Raj of what he needed to do to get permission to work. I also promised to pray for him, as he knew I was a Christian.

Then I did something which is unusual for any lawyer to do. On impulse, and perhaps because I didn't know how to comfort a crying man, I took out my wallet and gave him all the cash that I had. It was about $100. I told him it wasn't much but to take it and treat himself and his wife to a nice dinner that night. I also assured him that God was in control. The look in his eyes was of both surprise and joy — not so much about the money but knowing that a fellow human truly understood his pain. He had a very big smile on his face as he left my office.

Five years later, Raj and his wife finally had their day in court, and God was certainly protecting them, providing a compassionate Tribunal member to preside over their case. Somehow God softened the heart of this person to rule favorably despite all my doubts about the strength of the case. The decision to overrule the original adverse decision surprised me. Perhaps my own faith in God was lacking. In my mind, this positive outcome was nothing short of a miracle.

Raj and Parmita were finally granted their protection visa to stay permanently. Now they could take steps to bring over their only daughter, whom they hadn't seen for six years. Part of their suffering during the waiting period had stemmed from their initial decision to leave their young daughter with Raj's parents in India because they didn't know if they could take care of her while travelling in Australia. They certainly had no idea then that it would cause them to be separated for such a long time.

A year ago, when I returned to the NT for one of my regular business trips, I learned that Raj and his wife had started their own restaurant, so I made sure to drop by for a meal to congratulate them. Although it was only a new start-up business, I felt great joy to see how they had settled into their new country, how they were becoming valued members of their new Indian church. And the best news was that their daughter had finally been granted a visa to join them in Australia.

The Refugee

But there is a very interesting footnote to the above story. In April 2020, during the height of the COVID-19 pandemic, I received an interesting ABC News video clip from one of my NT staff. Raj was being personally thanked by the Chief Minister of the NT in a video hook-up for offering to provide free meals from his restaurant for local people who had been affected by the closure of local businesses. Raj explained to the Chief Minister that he felt compelled to help people who were hungry because Australia and its people had been good to him. His words moved me deeply, reminding me of the $100 I had given him in the darkest moment of his life and the ripple effect my small gesture of compassion had made through this man. One random act of kindness paid forward can sometimes go a long way.

A Small Giveaway
Jenine Altmann

It caught my eye. It stood on a narrow wall bench partially hidden behind the photo of a man dressed in military uniform. It was not an object I had expected to see in this particular situation. Maybe that was why it was partially hidden. I wasn't sure that I should bring attention to it. I decided to enjoy the meal before making that decision.

Ling, a small, elderly, Chinese lady, had prepared the meal. The small gas burner, steadied by pieces of wood, stood outside in the dingy alley. One of many alleyways that ran like rat warrens throughout this city area. Hundreds of one room dwellings opened their doors onto these alleys. A few privileged residents, cooking for tourist groups, earned extra money. The pungent aroma of rotting vegetables, stagnant water and crowded humanity affronted the nostrils. Temporarily, the aromatic smell of the meal cooking, overshadowed the stench.

While Ling huddled over her outdoor gas cooker we sat talking to our guide. There were few ornaments in this room. A two cupboard kitchen bench, a small shower/laundry cubicle, a bed, a table and three shelves were crammed into this single room. The wooden floor was achingly worn and stained by many years of foot traffic. A single-bed frame supported a sagging mattress and two thin blankets. A bare light bulb hung in the centre of the room.

The meal was testimony to Ling's cooking skills. Chicken dumplings, stir fried vegetables and fried rice were spiced to perfection. We talked while we ate. Ling told us about her late husband, experiences of her early life and something of her life now. We told her about Australia and why we had found ourselves travelling in China. Our guide was kept busy interpreting the flow of conversation. Ling talked about her husband, his life in the navy and the pride in the uniform. From her conversation it was obvious she loved him. When Ling brought the photo of her husband from the shelf, it exposed the small object I had seen earlier.

'I like that,' my husband pointed as he saw the object, too.

Ling smiled and took the well-worn little cross lovingly off the shelf. 'My husband and I have been Christians for many years. This cross reminds me of my husband and the faith we share,' Ling mused.

Ling's face lit up in wonder, tears glistened in her eyes, when we told her we too were Christians. The three of us prayed together and hugged each other. We acknowledged that while we would not meet on this earth, we would know each other in heaven. Our guide was amazed at the connection our shared faith had produced.

Was it a coincidence that led us to that particular alley to be fed by that particular lady? Are circumstances just chance? Whatever the reasons, all three of us felt blessed and thankful that we had met.

The Anthill

Diana Davison

I sat with my young daughter in the family garden. It didn't take long before I found my attention drifting towards a mound of earth gathered in the corner. The dark brown displaced heap of soil had meticulously been moved out from under the small rock that walled the flower bed. It had grown in size since I last noticed it the previous week. Like a busy shopping mall during the sale season, black ants scurried about frantically, as if looking for a bargain. They certainly had been focused in getting on with their machinelike mission of excavation.

I caught my daughter eyeing the ground lump. Inwardly, I was wondering if the developing anthill posed an issue to the area.

'Shall I get that sorted out when the plants next need pruning?' I asked gently, to gauge her response. I wanted to know where her mind was at.

'No,' she answered softly. 'It shows there is life…'

We both sat on the wooden bench in silence, taking a moment to observe our surroundings. Colourful flowers were in full bloom, smiling wide, inviting the bees. Various birds hopped from branch to branch, sending tweets about their business. Tall trees stood, patiently, offering shade away from the sun's heated glare.

Soon, it was time for us to go. With reluctance, we slowly got up in readiness to leave. We took turns to whisper our goodbyes, then left my father's grave to lay, once again, in the peace and still of nature.

I took my daughter's hand and we walked back to the car parked close by. She climbed into the passenger side next to me, buckling up. Driving out the gates, homeward-bound, I felt somewhat lighter, less mournful. My daughter has been able to handle the passing of her grandfather, with maturity. As for me, I too have bravely learned to weather this tempest. It has not been an easy two years. But now, I can see the bright peeking through beyond the gloom. I take reassurance in knowing, no matter what state we are in, we are never truly alone.

Suicide is not a Book in the Fiction Section
Isabel Barton

I don't know what the last sound my brother heard was. I hope that it was peaceful, as peaceful at least as a gunshot can be. I don't know what his shadow felt like, the shadow that plagued his conscience. What I do know is that his demons didn't die with him. They festered in those who lived on, those who survived. Death wasn't a cure; it was a poison. A venom which spawned lost secrets, secrets which clawed their way out of the grave and out of the ashes. The demons seized possession of us, my family, in our grief and our anger. But there was no priest to hold an exorcism and now the demons were a part of us, forever. We pretended that we were still under God's wing, but the hissing snake hiding in the trees became too loud and we were enraptured by his charming chant.

My name is Isabel and I am lost, yet I am found. I was born in 2003 and I have three brothers, but only two survive. When my brother Nick committed suicide my flesh stayed the same, but my soul changed. My heart shattered, and the wounds will never truly heal. I constantly peer into a broken mirror, seeing the world through the same eyes, but a different lens.

On the third of November, 2016, I was in my Year Seven food technology class. I remember that day, with all its anguishes, as if it was yesterday. I was making Rocky Road with my friends. Perhaps it was an omen of the rocky road that lay ahead. I was at the oven melting chocolate when a lady from reception asked me to pack up my bag, grab my trombone, and follow her. Blissfully unaware of what the future had clasped in its dishevelled grasp, I followed, like a duck following its mother across the road, oblivious to the oncoming traffic.

Led to a private room, my gathered items in hand, I stepped across the threshold from naiveté to realism. My dad embraced me. He was trembling, tears carving a path down his face, sobs racking his body. I thought my grandmother had died. Dad said he was sorry, but what consolation is sorry, when your twenty-seven-year-old brother commits suicide? The person I look up to, whom I admire. I do not use past tense when I say, 'I admire him.' I admire him not for what he did but for the life he lived, how he wore his heart on his sleeve.

I walked to the car, heavy, struggling to breathe, as if a carpet snake was constricting my ribs until the bones broke and my airways collapsed. There was also an emptiness at the same time. I had never felt true sorrow and loss before that moment. Ten minutes before the lunch bell we walked down the deserted corridors that would soon be filled with laughter, but where there was now only silence. The only sounds were lonely whimpers and silent screams. Silence can sometimes be louder than words. We left a river of despair with our tears wherever we walked that day. I was thankful that no one saw me so broken, but also fearful that no one ever would, that I would have to keep up this armour around me forever, hiding my vulnerability.

I am writing this because it is time for me to take off my armour.

I find that school is no longer a sanctuary, but a daily reminder of my new reality. I now notice how often people talk about death thoughtlessly. 'Why don't you just go kill yourself?' 'She looked constipated when she slit her wrists,' 'I should just go die in a hole.' School had always been a place where death was a joke. Perhaps because of our youth, death always seemed so distant that we began to fantasise about it, ignorant of its true finality and aftershock. I would like to say that I have been healed, but death is a wound that can't be stitched up. It leaves a permanent scar as a reminder for all eternity. Tragedy ripped through me with no remorse. In our family's grief the demon, Depression, came knocking on our door. We welcomed him in, and it has made its home in our hearts and will forever be a weight we bear.

So why do you need to know this? Why, because my brother's memory lives on through those who know about him, and I can tell you, he is worth knowing. He has an infectious laugh, one that can light up an entire room. Always up for an adventure. He has a heart of gold and a wild spirit. He lives a life of love.

I am telling you this because suicide is not a book that can be found in the fiction section of the library. For too long I have been in denial. I have been scared and ashamed, but this is not something to be ashamed of because without awareness and stories like mine, how can prevention occur? The claws of depression threaten us all; their touch cuts deep, drawing blood. My silent screams are now forming words. This is me saying what Nick never could. Don't wait until it is too late. Time is always of the essence.

Earth to earth, ashes to ashes, dust to dust.
In loving memory of my brother, Nicolas Michael Pope.

Graves to Gardens

Martina Kontos

Thump-thump-thump-thump…

My heart raced as I lay in bed, darkness enveloping my mind like a plastic bag choking an animal. I was running out of air, and fast. I gasped for breath, confusing my thoughts about death for death itself. My thoughts were no longer a separate entity, but I was them, and they were me.

Kill yourself.

Go on, kill yourself.

Don't you want your pain to go away?

For several months I had suffered anxiety and depression so severe that I had stopped going to school and was afraid to leave the house by myself. I had all but stopped eating due to a severe fear of choking, which had caused me to lose so much weight that my paediatrician had threatened to hospitalise me. My new depression was circling me like a vulture over its prey, waiting for moments of weakness to pounce. And, it knew that at night I was at my most vulnerable.

What's the point of living, when you're living like this?

What's the point of survival, when you're not even going to make it through the end of the year?

Night after night the voices returned. Question after question after question.

And then, one night, I again heard them whisper:

Kill yourself.

My breath hitched. I had never had a suicidal thought before. Yes, I'd thought about how life felt empty, but never to the point of considering suicide.

I closed my eyes and willed myself to go to sleep. But sleep didn't come, and the voices grew louder.

Kill yourself.

Do it.

End it already.

Then, the voices changed. No longer were they just thoughts, but they cut to my very essence. I felt inextricably connected to the voices. They understood my pain, the cyclonic darkness that my family had failed to notice. They understood me, because they *were* me.

Kill us.

You know that you want to end our pain.

Who can you think of that has suffered from multiple severe anxiety disorders, phobias, and depression at the same time, and survived?

No one?

Neither can I.

Do it.

I bit my tongue. I remembered learning about depression from a mental health worker at school. She had said that suicidal thoughts were unhealthy, and that we should seek immediate help if we ever experienced them. But in that moment, I couldn't remember why. I couldn't understand how someone could be so misguided as to suggest that people experiencing suicidal ideation *shouldn't* take their lives. Didn't I deserve to make my own decisions about my life? Wasn't it up to me to choose whether I got to live or to die?

I know that most people probably see suicidal thoughts as a violent struggle that a person has with choosing between death or life. But in that moment, the only coherent logic my brain could fathom was that death, and only death, would bring sweet, sweet relief. I was close enough to feel the whisper of death on my neck, and it delighted me.

If I was dead, then no more would I wake in the early morning from panic attacks that I couldn't control, heart racing so fast that I thought I was having a heart attack. No more would I stay inside all day, counting down the hours until night, only to remain awake as my soul ached for the sweet reprieve of a few hours of unconsciousness. No more would I drag myself around the house, my lack of energy from not eating leaving me almost misdiagnosed with chronic fatigue syndrome. No more would I suffer in silence, my family oblivious to the militant demons that controlled my mind.

As I lay in my cold bed, I thought about my family. About my mother, who would take my side even if I was to blame. About my older brother, who was like my own personal bodyguard, protective and caring. About my younger brother, who was quiet but would check up on me in the middle of the night to see if I was okay. About my father, who always said that positive thinking could overcome anything.

Anything. But this wasn't anything.

I was drowning in a sea of sorrow, the ashen waves lapping against my face as I struggled to stay above the surface. But what was I struggling for? I wasn't too sure anymore.

Although my family were oblivious to my internal struggles, I knew one thing for certain. No matter what I decided, I couldn't let them feel any pain. I imagined my grief-stricken mother dressed in black, standing beside my coffin, tears dropping onto the dirt, soul aching for the daughter she wanted back but barely even knew.

I silently screamed for someone to tell me what to do, what path to take.

And then, just like that, a small voice whispered one word — one word that would change the trajectory of my life forever.

Pray.

I curled up on my side and whispered with my last remaining breath of energy...

God...if you want me to live, then you're going to have to do something about it, because I'm done.

Soon after, I fell asleep, and the next morning my suicidal ideation had completely disappeared. It felt as if a dark fog was lifted from my mind, and I could finally think beyond the thoughts that depression had implanted.

Initially, I was more confused than I was relieved, and I questioned that the experience ever happened. Did God *really* answer my prayer? Or was this merely a momentary reprieve from suicidal ideation?

Alright, I told myself. *Everything seems better in the morning. I'll wait until night hits again.*

I spent the day worrying about my clear mind, afraid that by the time night fell it would again be smoked with chaos and confusion. When night did come, I climbed into bed and lay awake, waiting for the darkness to descend over me. I listened to my alarm clock ticking as I monitored every thought that passed through my mind, anticipating the suicidal thoughts to reappear at any moment. I was still depressed and suicidal, wasn't I?

I didn't have a single suicidal thought that night.

I haven't had a suicidal thought since.

Years later, when I went to Headspace, a government mental health facility, I shared my story and the clinicians marvelled. They couldn't believe that my suicidal thoughts had just disappeared. I knew that most of the workers there were probably non-believers, so I used the opportunity to tell them that the thoughts disappeared as a result of the power of prayer and of God. I know I planted a seed in that secular organisation, and to this day it makes me think of how God turns graves into gardens, as the song goes.

After all, he turned my grave turned into a garden of peace.

Slightly Awkward

Esther Cremona

The house was completely silent around me, yet a cacophony of words thundered loudly through my mind. 'Yes, no, maybe, maybe not. What if this happens or what if that happens?' The words played repeatedly in my mind. The fingers of my right hand danced lightly in the air, just shy of touching the computer mouse, while my left hand shaped into a loosely clenched fist. I had both eyes firmly focussed on the 'book now' button.

To click or not to click, that was the question. Return flights from Adelaide to Mackay. One adult and two children. Sole parent with a limited budget and a mild case of claustrophobia. Perhaps not so mild. Number 1 Daughter, the eldest child, had not flown since she was three years old. Number 1 Son, the youngest child, had never been on a flight. To add a little more of a challenge, I live with a rare, and progressive neuro-muscular illness. The illness affects my entire body, and I dearly wanted to embark on this trip while I still had some degree of independence.

Taking a deep breath, I clicked on the 'book now' button. A leap of faith that I truly hoped would come to fruition.

All sorts of scenarios played out in my mind. It was like a series of extremely short films, each with a different ending. Although I had taken both children on local holidays for several years on my own, this was pushing the boundaries of my comfort zone. Being divorced, disabled and a Christian has enough daily challenges. But God had supplied the strength to get me through the past several years; surely, he would take care of us during domestic travel.

The excitement of being able to visit family that we had not seen for several years was palpable. Family that lived on a secluded beachfront, approximately half an hour's drive from Mackay.

Holding my breath and half closing my eyes, I confirmed payment for the booking. My heart was racing but I felt that God would provide the strength and wisdom to guide me — I just needed to have faith!

The day arrived to fly. I slept in. Somehow I had bumped the volume to zero on the alarm clock. Number 1 Daughter came in at around 6.15 am and asked 'Aren't we supposed to be up by now?'

'Erm, yes. Yes, we are,' I replied calmly.

The calmness lasted about half a minute before the reality set in that we now had about half an hour to get ready and pack all the last-minute items. Flurried and hiding how flustered I felt from both children, it was a welcome miracle that we were ready on time.

Arriving at the airport, I was terribly nervous and also a little giddy with excitement at the thought of the journey ahead. Check in and 'priority' boarding went smoothly.

Number 1 Son was a little shaky. His face was expressionless, but his lips were just slightly pushed together — his unique way of shutting down to cope with stress. Number 1 Daughter had secured the window seat without opposition and exuded delight whilst we waited for the plane to begin its ascent.

The aircraft started to taxi down the runway and eventually whooshed its carriage into the sky. Although I had never been a reluctant flyer, I held my breath, closed my eyes and felt my heart thud-thud-thud rapidly against my rib cage. Nowadays, it seemed, I am not really that fond of take-off.

However, another member of my family is.

'Mum! Number 1 Son exclaimed exuberantly. 'That was the best feeling ever. Can we do that again?' I opened my eyes and saw his face beaming. Silently, I thanked God for the joy that both children now experienced travelling via plane.

We disembarked at Brisbane and searched for our connecting flight to Mackay. This time, Number 1 Son was pleading for the window seat!

Slightly Awkward

Arriving in Mackay was almost dreamlike. Me, just a humble soul — and a 'sole' parent, with physical disabilities to boot — had managed passage through busy airports, two kids in tow, poker face on overtime and a slightly forced smile to show the world. Smile and wave. Questions and prayers running on a loop through my mind each step of the way.

I felt we had almost made it. Then I faced a challenge. The tarmac at Mackay airport was a reasonable distance from the arrivals terminal. The staff advised it was a long walk and had arranged for a wheelchair. A wheelchair operated by a staff member to take me to the terminal.

I can't say I was terribly humble or immediately appreciative. For years, I'd been avoiding the thought of my condition deteriorating, most likely, to the point of requiring the support of a wheelchair on a routine basis. This would be the first time I'd resorted to using one.

My body language was not receptive, and my poker face slipped completely. I can only imagine how glacial my expression was when my voice came out with a definite 'No!'

Full credit to the experienced flight attendant who had the confidence to go behind the wheelchair and motion me in with a cheery, 'Well, just get comfortable and we'll have you with your family shortly. I'm sure you're keen to start your holiday and this is the best way to get you started.'

I could've resisted. I could've remained completely stubborn in my 'No' stance. Honestly, I didn't submit out of any genuine acceptance of needing the wheelchair.

Did I show good humour and agreement when I manoeuvred into the chair? No. I wanted to walk. Was it less stress for my body? Most likely. Did I have a moment of thinking 'Oh, this is okay, I can accept this'? No. My face most likely portrayed an expression resembling a disconcerted adult on the cusp of a mild tantrum, even though I was gracious and polite to the flight attendant as she wheeled me into the arrivals terminal.

We were all thrilled to see our aunt as it had been five years since we'd last met face to face. As we motored along the freeway to the beachside suburb of Mackay. I was in awe of the gorgeous countryside. Tropical plants and trees grew in abundance, and to see fields and fields of sugar cane in all its glory was to experience the fullness and beauty of God's creativity.

The house we were staying in was a new and purpose-built abode on a secluded beachfront. The beach and ocean were visible from each room of the house. Sand that was perfectly smooth in appearance, almost butterscotch in colour, silky and unblemished. The beach radiated as a golden glow under the Queensland sun. The ocean glistened and appeared to sparkle in places as it caught the late afternoon light. Gentle waves caressed the shoreline, sounding like a soft hush as the water met the beach.

The weather was forecast for the high 20s every single day of our week-long holiday. Completely perfect weather for fishing, swimming, kayaking, collecting fresh coconuts and beach walking.

Walking? Hmmm... Walking on the beach wearing dual leg braces and using mobility crutches is difficult. How was this going to work?

Well, if God got me this far, then he was going to provide the assistance, right?

He did.

My aunt and uncle proved a fabulous blessing. They encouraged me to remove my leg braces and walk barefoot on the beach. They would be nearby to support me, each step of the way. I hadn't walked barefoot on the beach for several years. Fear was overtaking me in several ways. Would I completely fail to walk without the braces? Would I fall? Would my children be so very disappointed? What was the worst that could possibly happen?

Slightly Awkward

I went full forward into that experience of faith. It was such a mixture of feelings when I felt that warm, soft sand beneath my bare feet. Such a simple pleasure to feel the balmy sun on my body, and to amble carefully towards the water along the shoreline. I can still recall the moment my feet were soothed all over by the temperate ocean lapping at my toes. Incredible.

No miraculous physical healing occurred. The rare illness I live with did not dissipate when my feet were bathed in the warm water of the ocean. However, God had brought me to a place where I could experience the fullness of his blessing, his strength in me, and feel his unconditional love.

There I was, and here I remain, slightly awkward — and winning at life.

The Perfect Song
Kaitlin Turland

The boat was buffeted by the waves because the wind was on it.[1]

My stomach churned like a tempestuous sea as the music teacher asked everyone to stand. The collective creaking of seats and shuffling of feet was accompanied by an expectant cheer from a few of the parents. The other singer adjusted her music stand and the drummer fumbled to arrange the kit to his perfection, but I stood still, suspended in my apprehension. The heat of the washer lights flooded my face, illuminating the air between me and the congregation into a surreal haze. It warmed my cheeks but not my clammy heart; it could not dim the terrifying reality of the next moment.

I breathed in with a forced depth, trembling with each exhalation, and counted down to the counting in. I scanned the crowd: the parents, teachers, grandparents, students, friends, classmates. Their faces dotted the large room as they watched in buoyant anticipation.

When he saw the wind, he was afraid.[2]

I had sung this solo in a dozen school assemblies before, usually passably, but not always faultlessly, so the perfection I required of myself for this graduation night wobbled like a newspaper boat on a choppy surf. What if I started in the wrong key? What if I sang out of tune? What if my tone trailed off into flat throaty dryness?

Four faint taps on the hi-hat broke the expectant silence. Next, the chord: my cue.

Shaky and unbalanced, I stepped out into the waters. I breathed in and voiced the first note, awaiting the reverberation of my lone singing through the church's sound system. Straining for the right tone, I sought the next note, my eyes fixed on the lyrics on the back screen.

---
1 Matthew 14:24 NIV
2 Matthew 14:30 NIV

Immediately Jesus reached out his hand and caught him.[3]

About to drown in my own self-absorption, I was caught by surprise. Instead of the echo of my own song, I heard the abundant resonance of 800 angelic voices, lifting a symphonious chorus of passionate praise. Utterly magnificent. The charismatic expressions of the joyful congregation outshone the dazing brightness of the stage lights, flooding the room with jubilant wonder. I closed my eyes as the perfection of the moment washed over my imperfect self.

Their enthusiasm supported the hand I could now raise up in freeing surrender. Free. Free to praise Him. I had been pulled from the waves of my own self-consciousness to lift my eyes to God. By his strength. For his glory.

'You of little faith,' he said, 'why did you doubt?'[4]

Raised arms formed sacred monuments established throughout the church. Unrestrained by bashful inhibitions, they sang with such passion and volume that I could barely hear my own voice and, most of all, I knew I didn't need to.

Jesus was our final word before we removed the music stands and exited through the curtain at the back of the stage. The song ended but the worship didn't.

And when they climbed into the boat, the wind died down. Then those who were in the boat worshiped him, saying, 'Truly you are the Son of God.'[5]

---

3   Matthew 14:31 NIV
4   Matthew 14:31 NIV
5   Matthew 14:32-33 NIV

The Crucible

Judith Noyes

People are going to rally around you…

Donna was relaxing on the back patio when the words flitted across her mind.

She was used to God speaking to her like that, so she tucked the words away.

And waited.

A few months later, Donna found herself in the specialist's surgery, with the results of her latest mammogram. The lump was cancer and she would need immediate surgery.

She had been down this path before, undergoing breast cancer surgery in her mid-thirties. She'd been healed back then, and we were all certain it would never return. Now, twenty-five years later…

The surgery was deep and complete. The surgeon didn't want to leave a single cell to multiply. Donna's body was scarred. Looking in the mirror, naked, she saw her heart beating where her breast once provided a protective cover.

You are going into the crucible…

Donna heard God speaking to her again. Was there more to face?

The stark, clinical walls of the oncologist's rooms were Donna's next place of waiting. He was a kind man but brutally honest. He told her she had a very rare cancer — only a handful of documented cases in the whole world. That it was likely there were more hidden cancer cells in her body. If the cancer didn't kill her, she might not survive the follow-up treatment. For twelve months, harsh chemicals would be pumped into her body, already weakened by disease and surgery.

Donna was sure she'd been healed back then. How could this be?

Then, again on the back patio, reading her Bible, these words jumped off the page:

Your faith is being refined by fire…

Donna pondered their connection with the crucible image, carefully storing them with the other words.

In living rooms all over Southeast Queensland, friends and family heard of Donna's new cancer challenge. And they began to rally around her. She had been living quite an isolated life as the carer for her adult son, but the isolation dissolved as she welcomed all the help she could get.

The next port of call was the Mater Hospital where a Power Port was fitted to allow the insertion of the chemical treatment into her body. It was a large, chunky device. While Donna was under sedation, it was inserted into a long slit in her side and took up residence under the skin in her upper chest. It felt painful when she woke and was uncomfortable to carry. During her seventeen cycles of treatment, she regularly had a long, large needle inserted through her skin to reach the device and dispense the chemicals. By the end of her treatment, the Power Port had worn a permanent groove in her bone.

Soon after its insertion, I visited Donna and saw naked fear in her eyes. I felt afraid as well. Donna had been taken to emergency with a very large clot in her neck, close to the main artery. The oncologist in emergency commented that it could be fatal.

I wondered if my friend would make it through all this.

But, as drugs were administered to break up the clot, Donna began to rally. She encouraged herself, certain that God had spoken to her. He knew what was coming. He hadn't deserted her. Then a further challenge presented itself.

In order to be discharged from hospital, Donna had to learn to inject herself in the stomach twice a day so the clot would keep dissolving. She cringed inwardly at the thought, but again she heard God speak, just a single word:

Resolve…

Certain now of God's caring involvement in her journey, she was able to self-administer the necessary needles to resolve the issue of the clot. This resulted in a black and blue and lumpy stomach which she bore with grace and courage.

It was around this time that Donna shared with me the words about going into the crucible. She wasn't looking for sympathy, but I was troubled.

Dear God, I thought... did you really say that? Hasn't Donna suffered enough in her life?

But she accepted the words, willing to have her faith refined. As she submitted to a year of intrusive, debilitating, painful treatment, she was buoyed by the words God had spoken. She became proactive, learning as much as possible about the administration of her treatment. Strong in mind and spirit, she sometimes found herself advising the new nurse on the ward regarding correct procedures for her.

One day, on the way home from another round of treatment, we visited the little Queenslander where Donna's ageing mother lived. She was dying. Her leukaemia had reached the stage where it was no longer subdued by regular infusions. I watched as Donna helped and encouraged her diminishing mother, ignoring her own physical weakness.

Not long after, as the people gathered in the chapel to farewell Donna's mum, everyone rallied around her again. There wasn't a dry eye in the place as Donna honoured her mother, delivering the eulogy with her head covered by a strange-feeling wig to hide her hair loss. Her courage extended to engaging with those gathered as they reminisced and ate a shared meal. This must have left her exhausted.

It was several months before Donna's treatment cycle was complete, and quite some time before her hair grew back, her wardrobe was replenished, and some strength had returned to her weary body. Slowly, Donna began to enter into normal life again, still within the constraints of being a fulltime carer.

She has now been cancer-free for six years.

And what of the crucible, that awful image that I couldn't bear to contemplate?

Before that terrible year, a soft sadness had always clung to my sweet friend — an overlay of melancholy that I thought dimmed her beauty.

Now, I call her my cheerful friend. So often, in conversation, our talk is punctuated by her merry laugh, sometimes when chatting about incredibly difficult experiences. Her laughter and joy are her most endearing characteristics. She was always thoughtful and kind, but it's evident now that she's been refined by her time in the crucible. My friend Donna shines brightly with a renewed faith and a fresh optimism she brings to each day, each person, each experience. I was worried that God was asking way too much of her. But Donna says that she feels cherished and valued by God her Father. Loved and nurtured more than ever before.

Post crucible, each new day is a gift from a loving God.

An Unexpected Adventure
Heather Gray

All week we had anticipated our visit to San Carlos on the island of Negros in the Philippines. We always enjoy our visits there where we have made many friends over the years. We had been there a few days and on Saturday Josue, pastor of one of the village churches near San Carlos, and his wife Melba had invited us, and our friend Alan, also from Australia, to their home in nearby Patunan, a lovely little village close to the sea. Their house is built into the side of a mountain, surrounded by lush rainforest extending all the way down from the mountains to the sea. It was a balmy afternoon and we had such a pleasant trip travelling there by jeepney, the vehicle unique to the Philippines.

Josue has an exuberant personality. When we arrived he told us he had a surprise for us. He wanted to take us for a ride in his boat and return us to San Carlos by sea. He had arranged for Dhong, a young lad who lived nearby, to have the boat ready. We were going out into the Tanon Strait which separates the islands of Negros and Cebu. It is a beautiful sight, looking across the strait to Cebu, the sea view broken only by Sipaway Island a short boat trip from San Carlos. However, before we left, Melba had prepared a lovely afternoon tea for us. We thanked Melba and said goodbye. Alan, maybe in his wisdom, had decided not to come with us and, as we were leaving, he returned to San Carlos with our friends in the jeepney,

The walk from the house to the shore was not far. We arrived to find the boat waiting for us on the sand. Two other young boys, Jezreel and Jake from a nearby village, were also waiting for us. Josue, the boys, and the two of us climbed into the small motor boat. Dhong pushed us out from the shore then he jumped into the boat, revving the motor into life, and we were moving away. The sea was lovely and calm as we headed east towards Cebu. The little ripples on the surface of the water glistened in the afternoon sun.

An Unexpected Adventure

It was not a long journey to the Port of San Carlos so we settled down to enjoy the trip. As we skimmed across the water we looked back towards the land to see the sun just starting to go down behind the tall palm trees on the hills beyond the sea on Negros. This gave a beautiful orange background to the trees that appeared almost black against the afternoon sun. The orange was now reflecting in the water. I was sorry I had not brought my camera, but as the sea began to be a bit choppy and splashed a little into the boat, I changed my mind and was thankful I had left it behind. I do have that lovely picture firmly fixed in my memory and do not need a photo to remind me of the scene.

A headland appeared in front of us as we glided along. We had to round this before we could see our destination, the Port of San Carlos. As we safely rounded the headland we could see Sipaway Island ahead of us. All seemed so serene when suddenly the motor began to splutter and choke. With a few more chugs and splutters, the boat came to a halt. We were adrift, without power, in the expanse of the sea. Josue seemed quite surprised about this and asked Dhong if he had filled the boat with fuel before we left. He said he had forgotten, assuming there would be enough in it. Josue then asked Dhong if he had brought more fuel with him, but he had not thought to do that, either. At this, Josue, usually so full of fun, was obviously expressing frustration, even though we could not understand what he was saying. His gestures and tone of voice told us he was not at all happy about the situation.

The sea was now calm and we were alone, too far from land for any one of us to swim even though we could see the island ahead of us. The boat was drifting here and there in the water, now dependent on the currents. The sun was beginning to set and darkness was coming in on us. There was not another boat in sight. Anxiety began to clutch at us. What were we to do? We certainly began to pray and ask the Lord for his protection for us all in this situation.

As we looked across the expanse of the sea, wondering what we could do in this small craft at night, we noticed another small boat appearing around the tip of Sipaway Island. We could see a man and a young boy in the boat. Josue stood up and began to send hand signals to them. We feared he might capsize the boat. As they came nearer he began to call to them in their language. What he was saying was a mystery to us. We sat there quietly, hoping and trusting that there would be some answer to this predicament. Across the water the two people in the boat now realised that we were in trouble. Their boat chugged nearer to where we were drifting and Josue was obviously able to indicate that our boat had run out of fuel. The boatman was able to tell Josue that they did have fuel which they could let us have. Josue conveyed this to us and also told us it would need to be replaced later so the man and his boy could return home. As the other boat came closer to us, Dhong jumped into the water and swam towards them. They handed their fuel can to him and he swam back to our boat, paddling with one arm and holding the fuel can above the water with the other.

Josue took the can from Dhong as he arrived back and Dhong clambered back into the boat. Josue filled the fuel tank and with a few pulls on the throttle our boat burst back into life. We felt a real sense of relief and gave thanks to God as Dhong turned the boat so it was again heading towards the port.

By now it was dark, but we could see the lights of the city guiding us home. Above us, the stars were twinkling in the night sky, a beauty we could now enjoy. Before long we reached the area beside the port where smaller craft could anchor. Other boats were already there, silent now after their day's activities. Many of these were outrigger boats that take residents and visitors to and from Sipaway Island. As Dhong manoeuvred our boat into a vacant spot, we could see quite a number of our friends waiting there to meet us. Word of our adventure had gone before us as so often happens here. We clambered up the bank to the roadway. Alan was there in one of the vehicles, smiling, feeling quite pleased he had not gone to sea with us. We were happy, though, that we were able to add this experience to our many adventures over the years. In spite of the unfortunate interlude, it had been an enjoyable trip.

Josue and Dhong now had to get fuel and return to the man and his boy who were out there waiting somewhere in the vast darkness. It was a pretty sight as the twinkling lights of many fishing vessels were beginning to appear on the now dark horizon.

Pastor William was waiting with a jeepney to meet us at the port and, as usual, a number of the young people were crammed into the back. Josue's brother was there too, as word of our adventure had also reached their village. Josue and Dhong jumped onto the back of his motorbike to get the fuel to take back to the other boat. How they were going to find the man and the boy out there in the darkness of the night we did not know. Next day, though, we heard that they did find them and all was well. Although some years have passed since this adventure, it is one we will never forget.

An Experience that Changed Me
Ellisa Thong

Since birth, I have suffered from many allergies; peanuts, eggs, food colouring, all types of seafood, and so many more. When I was a baby, all my parents could feed me was a few types of fruits. Going to restaurants or to dine outside had always been a pain. I usually would not be able to eat most of the foods served. Whenever I would go to family dinners, I would always feel like a burden. All my relatives would need to order specific foods just to cater to my allergy needs. When I was younger and my allergies were much worst, they did not want to order any seafood for they did not want me to feel bad that I cannot eat it.

There was an incident when I was 7 years old. I had a close-to-death experience with my allergies. I was not paying attention to my food and I consumed a frog! At first, I had not realised what had happened, but thirty minutes later, my throat started to swell. I could feel my airway slowly starting to close, and I could not breathe. In my mind, I started panicking and my relatives could see that the allergic reaction had taken place. I had to be rushed to the hospital immediately. During the whole ordeal, I was struggling to breathe but I was still conscious. I was really afraid of death and I was not ready to die. During the whole car ride, I was praying that the Lord will allow me to continue to live. Fear gripped my heart, but I decided to surrender it to God.

When I reached the hospital, they put me on a wide, blue gurney, and rushed me to the emergency room. All I could remember were my thoughts, telling myself I did not want to die. When I reached the emergency room, the doctor immediately injected a medicine in me and I lost consciousness. When I finally woke up, the doctor said that I had to stay in hospital for a few days for close monitoring. He also said that if I had gone to the hospital a few minutes later I probably would have died. I breathed a huge sigh of relief. I looked around and saw that my family was also there with me throughout the whole experience. It was a very scary time, but I knew I had the support of both God and my family.

I am very grateful and thankful that God still allowed me to live that day. He showed me how precious and fragile my life is. In just a split second, one could lose their life over the tiniest mistake they've made. This near-death experience was one that I will never forget. It taught me to live my life to the fullest. Even though I may still have allergies, I learnt to find joy in eating foods I could enjoy. People say that there are no second chances in life, but that night, I got my second chance, and I will not waste it.

A Timeless Symphony
Stephanie Taylor

The machines behind my father's hospital bed beep like a ticking bomb. His breathing staggers and wheezes. The light from the dark, cloudy sky filters into the room, making the faces of my family appear even more icy and grim. My dad probably asked for the lights to be switched off. He looks much worse than when I first left him to go to school this morning. I clench my hands together, determined not to show too much despair. I'm not even meant to be here. Right now my school recital would be playing. My guitar sits idly to the side of the room, out of the way of the nurses. That instrument should be playing. But it won't be tonight.

I tug the sleeves of my uniform further over my hands. Breathing in deeper, I try to imagine the musical melodies rippling across my school's auditorium. My father's staggered breathing begins entwining with the woodwind melodies. The brass instruments boom with the beeping of the hospital machines.

My heart beat begins increasing with frustration. I didn't want to listen to the sounds of this place. I didn't want to be here, full stop. But I also know that I can't be anywhere else.

I wonder if what rests before me is real. While I'm determined to detach myself in some way, I still can't look away from my dad lying there in this state. No one looks away from something they're still deciding is real or not. It's like seeing a friend or family member on TV, staring at the screen until you're 100% sure it's them. But even then, you half convince yourself it could be their double.

Shock, denial, repeat.

This endless cycle, or, what would seem endless and yet all the same instantaneous, feels like madness. Seeing someone so close to your heart slip from this world is madness.

A Timeless Symphony

The orchestra, still playing inside my mind, stops abruptly. No more woodwind. No more brass. I didn't even hear the heart monitor ring out that resounding, final bell of life.

Witnessing the sudden departing of a life is a sobering smack in the face. Nothing is quite as surreal as this moment. Dad's body is still here, but *he* isn't. How can we say he left us, when at the same time he hasn't? Stepping to the back of the room, I know he isn't here anymore. And there's no guess as to what part of him is gone.

Even at 17 years, I can see that something left my father. I have just witnessed proof that there's more to us than flesh. After this, how could anyone deny it? His very being is gone, yet his body is still here. Some might call it his spirit, or heart, but however you perceive it, the impression his absence left is profound.

Life doesn't end with death.

It is a timeless symphony.

Saved by Subtitles

Boo Hooi Khoo

It was May, 2019. Normalcy in our family was slowly being restored after three years of drama. From children's medical scares to loss of a loved one, God has been faithful. I was looking forward to some peace and rest in life.

But God was not done yet. My suppressed trauma, that I thought I had forgotten, resurfaced. My life was turned upside down again. I struggled with sleeping at night and getting out of bed. I no longer enjoyed being around others. There were days that I couldn't even get myself out of the house, and even when I managed to get out, I would put on a mask to hide my emotions.

My mental and spiritual health were not well. I was too embarrassed to seek help. My relationship with God grew distant as the days passed. I was in a dark place for some time. I struggled with self-condemnation. I could hear the devil telling me that I was not worthy of God's love and that I should not go to church anymore.

Somehow, for whatever reason, I still found myself going to church with my family on Sundays. However, I could not bring myself into the sanctuary. I could not bear to look at the cross in the sanctuary. I was ashamed of myself. I had so much excess baggage in my life. For almost seven months, I would stand outside the sanctuary and could not move any further. Most of the time, I ended up wandering aimlessly on church grounds.

Then the COVID-19 pandemic happened and our church services moved online. Out of nowhere, I suddenly had a desire to serve the Lord again. As a person living with severe hearing impairment, I was motivated to bless others by creating subtitles for our recorded church services.

In the process of creating the subtitles on Saturday nights, I listened to the sermon over and over again. In the quietness of the nights, I could clearly hear God speaking to me through the preacher's words. I was so overwhelmed by God's love that my eyes welled up with tears.

God helped me deal with my past through this subtitle ministry. I finally found my way back to him. God has shown me his grace and unconditional love. I can now confidently step into the sanctuary, look at the cross, and proclaim that he is my Saviour. He has saved me through the subtitles.

Palm Trees, Sand Dunes and Beach Umbrellas
Diana Davison

I was excited. My parents were going out of town and my father had offered to lend me his car during their absence. Amazing really, considering I had only held my driver's license for a few months. I was grateful for the trust he showed in me. A white manual Daihatsu that had many a mile under its belt, became my cherished chariot of choice to transport me around the small desert island we lived on. I was thrilled. Especially since it was the start of the weekend and, as usual, I had a busy social calendar planned. While the car keys were mine, I was determined to enjoy every moment behind the wheel.

Back then, on this small unassuming Persian Gulf Island, each Thursday was only a half working day before the weekend officially started. Friday was my Sunday. On this particular Thursday, I had arranged to meet up and hang out with a small group of friends. For me, as a young 20-year-old with more energy than most, the hours at work seemed to drag their heels as if concrete sandals were in fashion. Wearing the tedious hat of patience, while waiting and watching time slowly tick on, really didn't suit me. Finally, the minute hand rounded the office clock face to point at 1 pm.

My exit couldn't come quickly enough. I cleared my desk, grabbed my bag, and darted away as if the building was on fire. The thoughts of adventure and driving to meet my friends at the beach put me in high spirits, fuelled with reckless abandon. My vim and vigour sat on a full tank, and I was raring to go. Friends had planned to get together at a different beach. One which I had never been to, or heard of. This new destination added to the excitement. It was a beach at the end of a long stretch of desert driving. How I managed to eventually find this new secluded spot, God only knows. My sense of direction was definitely not delivered at birth, and in those days, on the island, there was not even a road map to follow, let alone a GPS navigational system. Palm trees and corner mosques were my usual land markers, helping me arrive at and find my way home from any given place, like scatterings of bread crumbs.

After a quick change into casual attire, I jumped in the car with beach gear neatly packed and ready to zoom. With the windows wound down, I had the music volume turned up to blaring. I was a young adult and I had the wind in my hair and freedom at my feet. Once out of the city, the road was empty and I was driving in the fast lane above the speed limit. It felt good.

With hands locked on the steering wheel, basking in my own company, I found myself momentarily distracted. Busy thoughts kept vying for attention. The road was under-active, but my mind was in overdrive. I wondered if my friends were on time and already there; how many were there? Who was there? I tuned back into the radio and knew I'd be there soon enough. I smiled at the sun that smiled back from the cloudless blue. The vacuous desert road encouraged me on, weighting my foot to the floor, speeding me towards this new oasis. The route, long and straight, was bare of any other travelling vehicles, or any form of visible life. The usual pockets of palm trees were scarce, with only a few to usher me on in-between stages.

Then, for no obvious reason, I decided to shift lanes. It was weird. With instant effect, I had a strange silent instruction in my head. I do not know what prompted it, but it was an automatic decision that had absolutely no thought behind it. However, in that split second of switching lanes, which I did without hesitation, I was taken by complete shock. The road had altered its face, as quick as sand does, and I didn't realise or see it coming. I was initially driving on a hard surface which had strangely veered off track. It was not a firm road anymore, but a deep inland sand dune, discretely consuming the road into its desert belly. In my preoccupied state, there was no need to change lanes. Why would I, when there were no other cars to be seen on this desolate stretch of road? Especially since I had been journeying in the same direction for some time. I was oblivious of any potential danger lurking ahead. It didn't take long to realise what had just happened.

It hit me like a bucket of iced water thrown at my face — stone-cold, sharp and by surprise. One major fact became apparent. The sudden need to shift lanes was not of my own volition. If I had not moved off the outside lane and into the middle lane at that exact moment, I would have crashed the car at high speed. No roadside assist or mobile phones back then. It dawned on me, in that instant, that I was not alone and my carefree spirit had been directed to safety. An invisible traffic warden had flipped my hourglass just before the immediate fall, allowing me to continue on through a narrow passage unscathed.

The rest of the journey was continued a few notches slower. I was nursing a sudden sense of guilt from speeding in my father's car. Questioning thoughts cried out in my mind. Why did I swap lanes at that precise spot? How many accidents had taken place on this road already? Was luck at play or something else?

At last, I reached my seaside destination to see a few plonked beach umbrellas flapping in the breeze like hula dancers in grass skirts. The salty water, with its gentle laps to shore, seemed to join in with the welcoming party of my splashing friends, who were beckoning me with their wet waving hands. I was relieved to see I hadn't missed out on much, even though I was the last one to join the happy gathering. More importantly, I arrived safely and in one piece. I have never forgotten that day. Forever thankful, I knew it to be a strange yet significant sign. A lesson learned out in the middle of nowhere and without warning. To this day, I am mindful of speed limits and to accept that we may not always see the hands that guide us on our path, especially when we least expect it.

In the Green

Liz Donald

Lying on the couch in my lounge room I look out white-framed windows facing south to the tops of bottlebrushes. All I can see is green and sky. As I take a breath, the trees seem to breathe too, inhaling and exhaling as they move slightly in a gentle wind.

Outside my bedroom window, facing west, the view is different but still green. Grape vines cling to the ageing fibro house next door, reaching down for our brown steel fence. In summer their leaves are vibrant lime, but in autumn they turn flaming red, burning against the background of brown and blue.

But it is the view out back and to the north that I love the most. Lush lilly pillies with pink new growth conceal the back fence and frame the view of the brick church behind our house. Terracotta pots stuffed with herbs and flowers surround the edge of our low, timber deck. In spring and summer the garden is filled with the sight and smell of jasmine, lavender, salvias and roses. Bursts of colour against the verdant green of the grass.

To the east the view is different. Through that window — the location of our house is laid bare.

Our house is perched next door to a large gravel carpark in the middle of a busy urban centre. Apartment buildings line our street. Weekdays bring swarms of shoppers making their way to busy restaurants up the road. The view out this window is one of dust and brick. Cement and metal. Brown and grey. For the first few years of living in this house I kept the blinds tilted down. I wanted to let light in, without having to look at the view.

My childhood was green. Or at least that's how it felt. I measured my height against an oak tree in our yard, each year finding it easier to grab the lowest branch and swing myself up into its boughs. Scrambling higher and higher, I stopped on the uppermost fork, the last limbs that could support my weight. I could feel the branches bending precariously with the effort of supporting me, but instead of feeling worried, the gentle movement from side-to-side made me feel as if I was a part of the tree, rooted on the edge of our gully in the Blue Mountains. From there I could see the whole valley stretching out before me. From the edge of our yard the land dropped away like the first dip of a rollercoaster, only to come up just as sharply on the other side. It was easy to sense God's presence there, up in the branches, overlooking endless trees and staring up to the sky. Black cockatoos would screech and fly off into the gathering dusk, the coolness of the air seeping into my skin and leaving a freshness that remained long after I had gone into the warmth of home.

But I moved away from my mountains home; first to study, then to work, live and start a family. I travelled far from the olive green of the mountains to the city, moving every year or two. I even lived overseas for a time, in a country where the mountains were brown and dusty, the air too thin and climate too cold for tall trees to grow. But throughout that time and all those moves I carried the memory of endless trees with me, as valuable as any physical item I possessed.

We finally settled, my husband finding a job as the pastor of a small church in a community that he loved. The people were warm and diverse and vibrant. The work was exciting and rewarding. The suburb was a densely populated, multi-cultural urban centre, full of life and delicious food. When we decided to move, we felt a sense of purpose — that this was the work God wanted us to do — the place he wanted to settle and put down roots with our young family.

And yet...

After a few months, the landscape of our new home began to unsettle me. I had always hoped I would make my way back to the mountains to raise my family. My eyes began to ache with a desire to see something other than brick and asphalt. Walking around my new neighbourhood, my eyes searched for the horizon, but I couldn't see it. Every way I looked my view was obstructed by another apartment complex; another brick wall. I felt uneasy. Out of place. Like I was trying to put down roots in a bed of concrete. I wondered if I was being petulant and fussy. Did it really matter if my new home was leafy and green? But no matter how many times I told myself it didn't matter, I couldn't stop the ache for my eyes to see green. Green that stretched to the horizon.

It was in trust that we began planting in our small backyard. First screening plants, to shield our eyes from the metal fence and metal shed in the corner. The effect was almost immediate — the green softening the industrial gleam, the harsh lines and sharp corners. We dragged concrete laundry tubs, abandoned under the house and planted them with jasmine and violas. A veggie patch followed. Then lavender by the back gate. Sweet peas to climb up the back wall of the house. For me it signified trust. Trust that we would be here to see and enjoy our garden as it grew and established itself. Trust that this would be a place we would experience God's presence with us.

Years passed and as the garden grew and put down roots, so did we, in our church and in the community. We even grew our family — another baby who has only known this place as her home. And through it all, my tiny garden, my sanctuary of green, became God's gift to me. It showed me that I am seen and known. God is gracious and will provide if we open our eyes and trust. We can put down roots and grow and thrive anywhere — if it is where God has placed us.

At some point I started opening my blinds that look east. The carpark doesn't seem so grating any more. From here I can see the movement of the town I have come to love. The elderly people congregating at dawn to practice Tai-Chi. The mothers strolling unhurriedly with toddlers in tow. The teenagers laughing and holding bubble tea.

I go out into my back garden and watch all the plants grow up around me. Climbing fences, reaching for the sky. It's dusk and white cockatoos screech in the lone gum tree next to a neighbouring apartment block. I look up from my garden at the changing colours of the sky. I feel the coolness of the air seeping into my skin and leaving a freshness that will remain long after I go into the warmth of home.

God is merciful all the time — and he gives us gifts, if we are willing to see them. He is there and I see his provision for me every time I look out my windows.

I see him in the green.

On the Way to Somewhere
Margot Ogilvie

'I'm sick of these four walls,' my client says when I arrive on a beautiful sunny afternoon to provide social support. 'I've got a letter to post, so let's go out. Where can we go?' Such indecision reveals the toll five weeks of COVID lockdown has taken. She's a strong-willed woman, and usually has a plan made before I even arrive.

My superiors recently complained when I clocked up 80k on an outing with this client, so I suggest posting the letter at the box across the road, then buying take-away from a local café. We can sit on a bench down the road, overlooking the seashore. Plenty of tourists drive a long way to do just that, when we're not in lockdown.

'Too close,' she argues. 'I want to venture further afield. Besides, that post box clears at noon. We've missed it already. This letter has to go today.'

'How about we see if Bob's Place is open for take-away, and find a park to sit in?' It's only fifteen minutes away and I know she loves Bob's Place. She was married to a Bob for nearly seventy years before he died ten years ago. It's been one of our regular haunts. As added incentive, I finish with a cheery, 'The sunshine is beautiful today.'

'No, we go there all the time... I know! Let's go to Finniss!'

'Isn't that a long way? They don't really want us to go too far, you know, with this virus business.' I'm not good at confrontation, especially against such a determined lady.

'Well,' she says, 'we won't be in a crowd. And besides, I'm going stir-crazy staying at home.'

I remember my training to treat clients with dignity and to respect their choices. And a recent reminder to care for our clients' mental health during lockdown. How can I say no?

Now all I have to do is find my way to Finniss.

'My sister used to live in Finniss,' my transformed client exclaims. 'I'll show you the way.'

I wonder how long ago that was. After all, she's in her 98th year, as she likes to put it.

As we drive, I begin to realise I've been conned. She talks about going by taxi to the hairdresser, yesterday. And to the chemist, bank and supermarket late last week. That's at least two outings since I took her out for coffee at Bob's Place this time last week. She's hardly house bound.

After fifteen minutes on the road, I slow down for a turn-off I know leads past a winery on the way to Finniss.

'No, not this one,' she says, 'I'm sure it's further on than this.'

I know there're numerous roads to Finniss, and she's enjoying being my guide, so I speed up again.

After a while, we approach a sweeping bend with another road going off to the right. There's a big green sign to Milang. I know we can get to Finniss down that road, but again she says, 'Keep going. There must be another road. We don't want to go to there.'

Further into the bend, a smaller sign says 'Finniss,' and, despite her continued protests, I slow down and make the turn. I'm certain we can find Finniss, then circle back on the winery road, minimising the kilometres whilst still doing her bidding.

We stop at the Finniss General Store and buy a coffee and a custard slice each. In the absence of clearance details on the post box, she opts to look elsewhere to post her letter. I explain, again, that we can't sit in the dining room, or at the tables provided outside.

'But there's no-one else here,' she argues.

'It's just the virus rules,' I counter.

'The problem is the fat between my ears,' she mutters when she remembers this is a global issue rather than a personal slight. 'It's solidifying.'

'We'll find somewhere nice along the way,' I say as I help her back into the car, although I'm not sure anymore where we're along our way to.

I try turning back the way we came, but she says, 'No, not that way. Let's see what's down this way.'

Every time we come across a turn-off, there's no signage. Unfortunately, I left my familiarity with this area back in Finniss, and am forced to rely on my navigator's advice: 'Stick to the paved road, dear. No need to take us on the dirt.'

'Perhaps we'll end up in Mt Gambier,' she says later, after telling me her family history, again.

I can't confidently argue otherwise, so I say nothing.

After what seems like forever, we come to a T-junction. Milang is apparently two kilometres to the right, Strathalbyn sixteen to the left.

'Let's go to Milang and sit overlooking the lake,' I suggest, certain I can still find that winery road and get us back on track homeward. 'Be nice to have our coffees soon before they get cold.'

For whatever reason, she still doesn't want to go to Milang, and makes that very clear, saying, 'I'd rather pull over and park on the side of the road than go to Milang and look over the lake.'

I turn left.

Every time I suggest a possible spot for our picnic, she turns it down. Our drinks will be cold. Our custard slices will be warm.

I'm hot.

I'm hungry.

I'm worried about the kilometres.

Finally, I just pull over in a little-used driveway, just far enough past the 'bags of chicken poo $5' sign so I can have the window down without a stench.

There's quite an art to eating a custard slice in the car whilst conducting myself in a professional manner. Fortunately, none ends up on my shirt, and I have tissues enough that I can use a few and still have some to offer my rather refined client, who seems to be really enjoying her afternoon tea.

Another glance at the clock and I'm enormously relieved my drink is barely lukewarm. I can gulp it down and get back on the road sooner rather than later. We're well over halfway through our time, and I have no idea where we are. However, refined ladies in their 98th year do not gulp drinks, and she doesn't want to drink it going along. It's all part of dignity and choice, I suppose, so I try not to look at the clock while I wait.

Finally back on the road, another ten minutes pass without us seeing more than the odd farmhouse. Then I spy an 80-speed zone sign. Surely it must be Strathalbyn. If I can talk her out of stopping, we might just make it back in time. I relax just a bit.

Until I get close enough to read the town announcement — Willyaroo.

I've been a local all my life and I've never heard of Willyaroo!

'My brother used to live in Willyaroo,' my annoyingly unflustered passenger tells me. 'It was a red-roofed place, I think.'

I don't offer to go looking for it. The only road I'm interested in is the one that takes us home.

It's not long before we come into Strathalbyn. Finally, I know where I am, even if it is still a monstrous forty minutes from home.

And yet another forty kilometres!

'Can we find the Post Office, dear?' she asks, indicating priorities far different from my own.

'I'm going to the Post Office back home after work,' I fib. 'I could post it for you there.'

Thankfully, that appeases her.

It's a sober ride home. My eyes spend equal amounts of time scanning between the road, the clock and the odometer. We're so far over the recommended 'don't go far' limit it's not funny, but there's nothing I can do. I have to get her home.

We turn into her retirement village at last, over-time and well and truly over-distanced. She almost seems repentant, I think, until she says, 'Would you mind detouring round the lake so I can collect my mail on the way?'

And of course, not being one to argue, and still striving for dignity and choice, I do just that.

My stress levels are high. I'll be in trouble again for sure. Then I remember a recent sermon along the lines of, 'Don't debate theology, just tell your story. No-one can argue with that.' So I debriefed in the form a story, pretty much like the one you've just read, and gave it to my boss the next day to read over morning tea. 'I'll be back with my timesheet later,' I called as I left the building.

When I dropped my timesheet onto my boss's desk later in the day, I still expected a reprimand.

'I loved your story,' she said, then glanced at my 100km fuel claim. 'Is that all?'

The Holiday
Nesta Hatendi

The last five months have not been how I envisaged them before I left home. I arrived in Australia in March for a family reunion and a once in a lifetime trip to Bali, thrown in as a bonus. I was very excited to stay with my two daughters and their partners in Sydney after a year's absence.

Organising the trip to Bali had started months before online. We wanted an island destination since my children and I have lived for most of our lives in a landlocked country. We had romantic dreams of a small paradise where we could live a life of decadence with exotic seafood, boat rides, culminating in a memorable tropical experience. Sunbathing was not on our to-do list since we were born with a natural deep tan.

We had ruled out the Maldives and Seychelles with their expensive lodges and unique attractions and settled on geographically close Bali, said to be reasonably priced with a lot of positive reviews as a popular Australian holiday destination. The island was drawing us to its shores, the Land of the Gods, with its breath-taking natural wonders, 'looming volcanoes and lush terraced rice fields' that exude peace and serenity.

My family prides itself in being highly efficient organisers who believe in a future open to all sorts of possibilities. So we had bought our airline tickets, well in advance, when prices were reasonable. We planned to stay in a sizeable beachside house near perpetual rolling waves. The whole family had unanimously selected the property after being given a picture preview of its luxurious expanse on our Whatsapp group, optimistically called 'Future Family Holidays'. We had even roughly planned each day's schedule, sightseeing trips and a cooking roster of delicious meals. Our holiday packing was going to be determined by the selected daily activities. Some were planning to exert themselves and would be spoilt for choice with scuba diving, walking trails, swimming in the warm Indian Ocean. Others envisaged walks galore along the beach and reading books set aside for just such an opportunity. Who could want anything more? Sun, sea, sand and exotic cocktails with family on a tropical island!

In contrast, I had just transited through a grey London with its perpetual early spring drizzle, unpredictable temperatures, crowded underground and majestic historical buildings. I have a soft spot for London. However, a tropical paradise sounded idyllic after a long haul flight through Dubai. Ominous news headlines in the media were beginning to spread infectious anxiety about an unknown disease. Conspiracy theories were gaining momentum concerning an epidemic coming out of Wuhan, Hubei Province, China. A containment strategy had gone wrong, spreading an unknown illness of biblical proportions across the globe.

A long-time friend in London had been keeping me posted about these new developments when I was still in my home country, even before the virus had become a source of disquieting headlines. She had international consultancy contacts as well as friends in WHO and other disease tracking organisations and her text messages and telephone calls during my stay in London had become increasingly alarmist.

'When are you leaving the UK? Have you heard about the imminent border closings where you are going? When will you arrive in Australia?'

I initially thought she was overreacting and stayed complacent, with no real sense of urgency. My flights were booked, and I had fortunately experienced no problems while in transit.

A few days after arriving in Sydney, March 25 to be exact, while I was still experiencing the euphoria of the family reunion and recovering from my jetlag, we heard that all citizens and permanent residents were now prohibited from travelling out of Australia, without an exemption. Airlines were now prioritising returning residents who were being encouraged to come home before international borders closed. I started to realise that I was one of the lucky ones. Unlike others, I was at least not stranded in a transit hotel of a foreign country, not knowing whether I could fly.

The long-awaited Bali holiday dramatically smouldered into ashes as news headlines referenced new visa restrictions to limit the spread of the virus in Indonesia. The global epidemic was now a pandemic which had a name — COVID-19, spreading like wildfire beyond the Chinese borders. A domino effect had started as the flight cancellations increased daily and travel agencies began casting doubt about insurance cover, ticket and accommodation refunds. Governments were moving into emergency mode at various paces, preparing for the unknown. I felt as if I had dodged a bullet as I read of the near media hysteria spreading in the UK and beyond.

I began to move in and out of despondency as the expiry date of my three-month visa was fast approaching. My increasing concern was that I would breach my visa's maximum three months stay and jeopardise any future applications to re-enter Australia. My airline had also emailed saying my booked flights were now in limbo after being cancelled twice. Panic mode kicked in, in earnest, when it advised that it did not know when regular flights would resume.

Sometimes, when uncertainty mixed with despair is at its worst, and you feel you are reaching rock bottom, that is when the unforeseen happens. Out of nowhere, I started getting news from multiple sources that visitors stuck in Australia because of the pandemic, could apply for a bridging visa so that they could stay legally in the country.

I recall the palpable relief when my family helped me to locate the nearest Immigration Office with the shortest processing list. I had already applied for a visa extension online. After driving ninety-seven kilometres out of Sydney, we arrived at the processing office which was busy with a continuous succession of family members arriving to take medical examinations in support of their online applications. Old, anxious parents who needed English translators came with their resident children and citizens were applying on behalf of visiting partners.

After completing the medical process, there was a wait of 40-45 days for a response. A long wait. However, it was better than staying illegally in a country that is not my own. I had the means to apply for the visa and family members to provide unconditional support. I also realised that, as a family, we have not been together, in the same country, for such a long time — even though my daughters are in two different states. It had now become an unplanned extended holiday, at the mercy of COVID-19 restrictions. The only downside was the limited touristic places to visit.

In May, I crossed over to Victoria to live with my eldest daughter and her family. It was a long nine-hour car ride, and an opportunity to bond and sightsee while passing through rolling scenic countryside. I was fortunate to cross from one state to another before state borders closed.

As a proud owner of a valid transit visa, I now feel as if I am in a safe bubble, even though live media updates continue to bombard us with gloomy headlines of daily global numbers of deaths in new hotspots. We have even internalised new catchphrases which pepper our conversations-social distancing, PPEs, working from home.

It is currently the turn of my nation to be overwhelmed by a pandemic wave of panic, contagion, death and despair. Most country borders are still closed. The airline, from which I bought my return tickets, has not yet opened up the skies to fly home. Yet despite these unpredictable times, I feel an overall sense of relief and am at peace, in an intangible place of safety and security.

My Two Mothers
Donna Meehan

This is the story of my two mothers.

My birth mother's name was Beatrice and she had eleven children. The first seven were taken by the government in 1960. My mum was told they sent me to New Zealand. The government finally apologised to the mothers for all the lies they told them. I stood with my two brothers at the National Apology at Parliament House in 2008, representing our mum.

Mum came from a proud Aboriginal family, who spoke their language. She was gifted with the most amazing voice, winning eight singing competitions in far west New South Wales. Mum forfeited first prize, which was to travel to Sydney to record her own LP record. She was invited to sing before Queen Elizabeth at the opening of the first Sydney Entertainment Centre, but she refused to leave Coonamble as she didn't want to leave her four other children. Mum's love for children came from her broken heart, of living without her first seven babies. Her home was opened to all children, who she always gave a feed and sung to sleep with her tender voice. They called her the Patsy Cline of the West.

I met her in 1979. My two mums met a few times and thanked each other for caring for me. I enjoyed six years of contact, but sadly Mum's life was cut short when she passed due to a heart attack aged fifty two. I remember my adoptive mum sitting at her dining table saying 'No Lord. Please take me and leave Beatrice for Donna. She needs her mumma.'

How does one describe love? It is like a prism with thousands of different colours. A love for every situation in life. So often taken for granted, love is fragile and yet so strong. You could never paint a picture of something so spiritual, liberating, binding and eternal.

Life is like a melody softly and sweetly played like tinkering notes on the piano.

I held a secret fear in my heart for over thirty years, the fear of my loving adoptive mum dying. I couldn't imagine it. I wouldn't be able to let her go too. How does one prepare for that crescendo in life? Usually, when we get to the end of our tether, we find that God is there, waiting all the while. He waits in the darkest places, in the midst of the darkest night. I have often knelt before him and laid my head in his lap and cried like a four year old child.

When my eighty-eight year old adoptive mum was diagnosed with dementia, I had been a widow already for fifteen years. I was an only child who had been lovingly adopted, a member of the Stolen Generation. My colour was not an issue for Mum. There was just Mum and me in all of Australia. We had each other. So the thought of losing Mum was breaking my heart. I wept before the Lord and asked, 'Who will love me when Mum goes?'

God said, 'I will'.

Again I asked as I thought God did not hear me.

Again he replied, 'I will.'

'Oh yes, Lord, of course you will,' and I closed my eyes. When I opened them it was morning.

The dreaded day came when Mum had to leave the hospital and be admitted into an aged care centre. I had wept all night. How does a daughter take her mother to an aged care centre, when all she had known for over thirty years was her little two bedroom home. I walked inside to find Mum smartly dressed and wearing a big smile, her eyes dancing.

Mum asked, 'Where are we going?'

'For a drive and to get a cup of tea,' I said.

As we had done every weekend for the last five years, Mum sat in the front seat, looking at the shops as we drove down the main street. God turned up on time, as he always does. Mum fell asleep before we got to the end of the main street, and I drove for forty five minutes, playing hymns and singing the way.

When I stopped the car Mum said, 'Oh are we here. Are we going for a cuppa?'

'Yes, Mum.'

Only a loving God would make my hardest tasks so easy. I dreaded the moment when Mum would no longer remember my name.

Late one night, five years later, I read Isaiah 49:15: 'Though a mother may forget you, yet I will never forget your name' The very next day, when I walked into the aged care centre, was the first time ever that Mum hadn't recognised me. Normally, that would have shattered me, but God had prepared me and gave me a verse of hope. Ten minutes later Mum realised who I was.

As a young woman, Mum was trained in the opera and had a soprano voice. I grew up with her singing hymns in the house. Even in her eighties Mum could still sing. Now in her nineties every once in a while I would hear her softly singing along with the hymns. I cried as it brought back memories of a gifted singer, and I would think that would be the last time I will ever hear her voice, but then a few months later I was blessed again to be able to hear her gentle, tiny voice.

We celebrated Mum's 100th birthday. Then three months later, while I held her hand, she gracefully fell asleep and woke up in Glory. My heavenly Father never failed me. I had not wanted Mum to pass alone. I wanted to be there, just as Mum had always been there for me. God made that moment possible. His timing is absolutely perfect. That precious moment was peace-filled and dignified.

Days with dementia are like walking in a dark forest. I have learned that in the shadows some lovely flowers grow. In the darkest hour comes rays of hope, rays of sunshine, dew drops of grace and sprinkles of strength.

Today is an empty page, yesterday is gone, tomorrow's page has not yet been written. Allow God to write in the blue print of his love: '*Fear not. I am with you. I go before you. I know when you sit down and when you stand up. I will bless you and keep you and make my face to shine upon you, be gracious to you, lift up my countenance upon you and give you peace*' (Numbers 6:24-26).

I am not alone. I have been adopted by God.

Unexpected Grace
Kylie Gardiner

It's one of these homewares shops where everything sits perfectly. Beautiful table settings — all matching bowls, utensils and colourful runners, serviettes folded into glassware, and carefully arranged flower displays. There are large cream and white couches bursting with perfectly toned cushions. A glass cabinet sits near the front counter filled with pearls, earrings and glowing treasures. Huge vases sit upon long sideboards and dining room tables. Stacks of artificial flowers and stems are tucked away in corners. Shelves to show off 'look at me' pieces. Mirrors reflect the lush interiors. Different scents waft and follow you throughout the maze of furniture. And below the main floor is a basement — an Aladdin's den of rugs and carpets.

My four-year-old and I survey this magical world. Can we navigate our way through? There is a wooden magazine box that attracts my attention. It is the perfect colour for our lounge room. The desire to acquire entices me in. My hand grips my daughter's tightly. We have the conversation of looking and not touching. She is old enough to obey this instruction. I stop on my way through when a wooden sculptured boat takes my attention. Expensive. I carefully sit it down again. I look for the hidden price tags as we make our way through.

Above the shop on the mezzanine level a tall lamp shows off its stand, a knotted wooden trunk, and it shines its light on a huge Maori warrior shield set at the back. It is at least six-foot-tall and two foot wide. Glossy wood with the carving of a face embedded in it. A noble hunter's defence. A detailed artefact from another country and another age. It's great hulking presence looking down on the shop.

The magazine box is there too and my eye goes straight to it. I let go of my daughter's hand as I pick it up and turn it over to see the price. Two hundred dollars. For a magazine box!

Disappointed I place it back. The sales assistant sees me put it down and, as if reading my thoughts, calls out to say it is high quality reclaimed wood. The older it is the more you pay I think to myself. While we are talking a little hand pokes at the warrior shield — fascinated by its vastness. She moves away and then it falls. A massive crash that shakes the floor. The furniture shudders around it. The sales assistant lets out a squeal. The six-foot monster lies on the floor. It's fallen backwards and its grotesque face looks up at me. My daughter stands there stunned. We both know we are in big trouble. I'm so thankful she is alright but almost simultaneously is the fear of what is going to happen next. I was bracing myself for a severe telling off. Going on the prices in the rest of the shop this shield must be worth thousands. The sales assistant is the owner and she runs towards the stairs to us.

'I'm so, so sorry,' I say as she hits the first stair. Here it comes. I expect anger, yelling and an enormous bill. The voice in my head condemns me with phrases like 'what were you thinking bringing a child into this store, you could have killed her' and 'what kind of terrible mother are you!' I'm going to be black listed from this shop forever. And then the owner speaks.

'Oh sweetheart. What a shock. Such a big bang. Are you okay?' She squats down to my daughter's level and hugs her. Something I'm ashamed to say I hadn't done — too caught up in my fear of the consequences.

'And how's Mum?' She stands and rubs my arm.

I trip over my apologies. There aren't enough ways to say sorry.

'Well let's see what the damage is,' she motions to the shield.

I'm almost too scared to look. We grab either side of the wooden mask and, struggling, push it upright against the nearby railing. Miraculously it is still in one piece. Not a chip. The relief is overwhelming. I run a trembling hand over my wet brow. My daughter is so shocked by the noise and the reverberations she hasn't thought to cry yet, but now a few whimpers are released. I gather her into my arms. It hits me how incredibly grateful I am that she hasn't ended up underneath this mammoth object. It could have been a horrific scene.

'Thank you, God,' I whisper into my daughter's ear. Then I brace myself for the full dressing down. I deserve a telling off. I did the wrong thing in letting go of my daughter's hand. I didn't look around enough to see what were the threats. I can feel the tears coming.

My emotions take me back to my own childhood. At a similar age I accidentally knocked over a tin of paint off a builder's scaffold that I'd been given strict instructions not to touch. But I went to pick up a brush that had fallen down and the handle on the tin caught my clothing and tipped over. I got a stern rebuke and a hiding. Now that same fear consumes me.

'I will pay for it all — for any damage that's been done. I should have realised it wasn't safe.'

'It wasn't a very good place to display it, on reflection,' she says. I am still waiting for her to haul me over the coals and black list me from the store forever. Instead she motions for me to sit down on a nearby couch.

'It's all fine, there's no damage. Now don't go telling yourself off' (she was a mind reader too). 'Accidents happen. The most important thing is that everyone is okay. We can always replace the furniture but we can't replace you,' she says, looking at my daughter.

I feel the burden lift. My spine straightens. I can hardly believe this woman's response. Her concern for us is genuine and generous. I expect anger and stern rebukes. I receive care and understanding. She speaks of her own memories and of how hard it is keeping tabs on a young child. I'd taken my child into a shop that probably wasn't designed for children. I'd let her slip from my grasp for just that amount of time for disaster to strike.

'Why don't you just stay there for a bit,' she says.

'Thank you, thank you so much.' She can see my shakiness. As we sit my heart beat slows and the tears dry up. My daughter puts her hand into mind and I squeeze it.

It was a lesson in grace. To receive the exact opposite to what I expect was a soothing salve from God. He is very close and it calms me. And it makes me determined to pass on this grace to someone else when the situation arises. Grace is like that — it's a gift received, and a gift to pass on.

The Kodak Moment
Stephanie Taylor

I felt so prepared for this expedition. No one was looking forward to the two week trek across the Victorian Alps more than me. I thought to myself, 'Daily hiking? Sweet, I love to travel,' 'Carrying everything you need on your back? No problem, I've been training with my school bag for ten years now,' 'No phones? Easy, mine is practically a brick anyway.' Nothing was going to slow me down. And I was determined to share this enthusiasm with my friends.

'Can you believe the day has already come?' Rachel asked, leaning over the bus seat with bulging green eyes. She always had a flare for the dramatic.

'It's crazy,' I nodded. 'I don't know why, but I thought I'd be older. All the other Year 9s looked so mature when we were growing up, but I still feel like a kid.'

Rachel grew pensive, 'And I thought I'd be fitter. There's no way we've had enough training. I still can't finish our running circuit without needing to walk some of it!'

'You'll be fine,' I reassured her. 'Besides, it's just hiking, not a 400m sprint.'

She raised her eyebrows with a pointed look. I knew what that look was for. It wasn't just any hike, it was a 20kg backpack trek through the mountains. But I still shrugged it off. Surely she was just overthinking it. It really couldn't be *that* bad. And yet, despite how long and tedious the expedition was feared to be, it was only the first day that proved to be a true shock to the system for me.

As the bus pulled up to our starting point at Telegraph Junction, we set out in the pouring rain. Fog rolled over the track, filtering everything in sight with a white tinge. Our hands stung from the icy temperature. I wished that I'd packed my gloves last, and not first where they sat at the very bottom of the pack. It was still raining when we finally arrived at our campsite. This made it incredibly difficult to set up our tents without getting them too drenched. We were all struggling, but I found it particularly difficult to keep my hands from shaking so much.

'No, I didn't bring a hot meal for tonight!' I snapped at Rachel, who had merely asked what I was having for dinner.

My friend and our teacher, Mr. D, exchanged a knowing look. Their eyes monitored my uncontrollable shaking hands and temper. I could practically see the list of symptoms for hypothermia being ticked off with their eyes. Mr. D. spoke to the other teacher in our group, and it was agreed for me to be promptly ushered into an overcrowded, two person tent for warmth.

While the other members in our group stayed up to share their experiences of hiking on the first day, Rachel and Izzy remained in the tent with me. Neither of them seemed the least bit concerned about missing out, and instead made sure that I was doing okay. My bad attitude was quickly silenced by their willingness to look out for me. A few other members of our group checked in with me, and made suggestions of ways to keep warm. All I could say was thank you because, truthfully, I was embarrassed. This trip wasn't meant to be this difficult. *I* wasn't meant to find this so difficult. My pride was getting in the way, but I began to realise I hadn't prepared for the trip very well. The Victorian Alps was very different to our air conditioned lifestyles at home. I took up the advice to wear a beanie to bed, and eventually drifted off to sleep.

The next day, the early morning frost bit at our skin, reminding us of the wild landscape we had settled ourselves in. My hypothermia had subsided, and while I had developed more humility, I was still grouchy from the cold. I wanted to excuse myself by telling Rachel I was never a morning person, but she knew me better than that. Instead, I complained to her about how icy the metal poles and pegs were. It was impossible to coordinate the pack down of our tents with gloves on; they were too restrictive. But the moment our tents were packed away and on our backs, the gloves came on quicker than a scurrying gecko.

By midday, however, no one could wear anything but shorts and a T-shirt. We learnt to read the cues of approaching weather, because even before coming on camp, we were constantly reminded by our teachers that there wasn't going to be any heating or cooling systems. We all rolled our eyes after hearing about it so much, until we actually had to deal with the unpredictable conditions. And so, on particularly cold mornings with a lot of fog, you could almost guarantee it'd be a hot day once the sun burned through the clouds. If the morning temperature was a little warmer, generally there's been more cloud cover overnight and virtually no fog. This would mean the rest of the day would continue without much sun and wouldn't be as warm, as opposed to a morning that started out a little frostier.

The time of day even became less of a mystery despite having no clocks. It was easy enough to distinguish lunch time. Not because we were hungry, we were always ready for that bag of scroggin, but because the sun was directly above us. By late afternoon, we wanted to know how much time we had left before the sun went down. Setting up tents in the dark wasn't an easy task. Lining up the palm of the hand with the horizon, each hand width up to the sun equals another hour until the sun sets. With just one hand width from the horizon to the sun, it equals one hour left before the sun sets. This practice became as common as checking your watch for the time.

After a week of reading the cues around us, I and my group had developed a far more appreciated respect for our surroundings. We realised how much we thought the world had revolved around us, or our preconceived expectations of what we thought we should be able to do. Collectively, during our campfire discussions, our group of fifteen year olds began to change how they thought. It went from, 'It's too hot or cold. It should be *this* temperature,' to 'It's this temperature. I should wear and pack this for the day.' Inevitably, we began to think less about ourselves, and more about others. The more we spent surrounded by creation, the more appreciative we became about the bigger picture.

This concept crept into our campfire discussions throughout the expedition, but particularly towards the end of our stay in the bush. The 'Kodak moments', as our teachers liked to enforce, prompted us to consider something about our trek that caught our attention.

'The sun slowly set over the horizon while I was unpacking the tent, and just like that, I had to stop,' one of the boys explained to us. 'The hills stretched out so far it went beyond the horizon, and it kind of leaves you struggling to find a reason why God doesn't exist. It's just so... big.'

I was captured by the appreciation these boys had. But I was never going to admit that, not even during 'Commending time'. However, I couldn't agree more. If someone told us that the moss which glimmered along the creek from the morning dew was a fluke of atoms, I'd be more suspicious at the odds for such repeatedly random beauty. The longer we spent away from the world of man-made buildings, lights, roads, air-conditioning and even clocks, the more we stopped believing that we had built the world, or that the world revolved around us. We truly were just a grain of sand in the midst of a vast desert, not a collision of random atoms. The uncertainties and troubles in life suddenly felt so much smaller when we returned home. And our mindset toward others and appreciation of God's creation had grown as a result.

Sprinkled with Surprises
Liisa Grace-Baun

As we ascended from Adelaide airport it was hard for me to contain my excitement, knowing that in less than twenty-four hours we would be landing in Finland, my homeland!

This is where my story began.

At the age of seven months I had been abandoned by my biological mother, Marjatta, and went to live with a Finnish foster family until I was four, before being placed in an orphanage when they migrated to Australia. A year later, my foster mum, Laila, discovered I was in an orphanage; up until this point she thought Marjatta had taken over my care. Laila then adopted me and I migrated to Australia to be with her.

After my mum Laila passed away I developed a deep desire to return to my roots and spend some time in the country that was home to her for over forty years prior to her migrating to Australia.

I expressed to my husband Dave how much I wished I had found my older sister before this trip, with the hope of seeing her. We shared the same biological mother and had both been adopted to different families. I last saw her when I was around six months old.

I told Dave how I had searched for her on Facebook and found several people with the same name as her; however each person replied with, 'Sorry, you have the wrong person.' Dave asked if I had tried searching her name on Google. As soon as I did, her business profile came up with a photo of her and where she worked. So, just a few hours after arriving in Finland, I emailed her at work with the subject heading: 'Your sister from Australia.'

I kept checking my phone to see if I had an email reply from her. Later that night I was literally breathless for a moment when my phone started ringing. The call was from a foreign number that I didn't recognise, so I knew it had to be her. Answering the phone, I was greeted with, 'Liisa, I received your email today which I read and re-read over and over again.' It was so wonderful to hear her voice. Neither of us were lost for words as we speed-balled our lives into a nutshell. We spent well over an hour lost in conversation and making plans to meet before I left Finland.

That night, as I lay my head down, I thanked God with all my heart for blessing me with something so unexpected.

On that first day in Helsinki I also messaged my biological brother Asko and sister-in-law Milja, to let them know we were in Finland, and they too were eager to see us. The last time I saw my brother was thirty years earlier, when I went back to Finland to meet my birth mother and siblings.

On day three of our travels we caught a bus to Imatra where I was born. Tears welled within and my stomach churned as I thought about my biological mother having given birth to me here. Feelings of rejection threatened to engulf me, yet again; however I was reminded of how God had healed me of all the past trauma during my early years. As I reflected on that, I felt the warmth of his love and healing again.

We captured every opportunity possible to enjoy a sauna and swim in the lake. It was that feeling of 'home' and as though I could taste the culture.

Friends of mine offered to take us anywhere I'd like to go.

I asked how far the drive would be to get to Virojoki, which is where my adoptive mother's parents were both buried and where I had attended Sunday school for several years. As it was only a two-hour drive away we were able to do this trip. As soon as the church came into view I remembered it. 'Yes, this is it!' I squealed, 'this is the church where I attended Sunday School.'

We began searching for my grandparents' graves and then noticed a lady pushing a wheelbarrow. Calling out to her we asked if she happened to know where the graves were, giving her the names. She smiled and said, 'Oh yes, that is my godmother's grave, I'll take you there.'

'Wait, did you just say that my grandmother is your godmother?' I asked.

'Yes, that's right,' she responded, still smiling.

There were so many graves that without bumping into the woman with the wheelbarrow it would have taken us hours to find my grandparents. As we stood there at their graveside, she told stories of my mother and grandmother. I couldn't believe that this lady was connected to my family.

It suddenly occurred to me that if she knew my family then she would no doubt know where I lived with them as a child. She certainly did, and was able to give us directions on how to get there.

As we were driving down the road where I had lived with Laila and my adoptive family prior to migrating, I could sense the house was nearby even though we had driven the whole length of the road and hadn't found it yet. I asked the driver to turn left at a driveway that veered off from the road. As we pulled up in the front of a big old two-storey house my heart was bursting.

'This is it, this was my home!' I exclaimed.

We knocked on the door but nobody was home. Initially I felt a little disappointed and then right at that moment a car came driving into the driveway. I walked over to the young lady and asked if this was the house where my family had lived almost fifty five years ago, and with a surprised and curious look on her face she replied, 'Yes.'

She invited us inside and there in the kitchen was the old stone oven where my mum had spent hours every day cooking and baking. I could visualise myself sitting there as a little girl watching her.

I made my way upstairs and there, too, I had the warmest feeling as I looked at the walls that still had the original wallpaper.

After taking many photos I thanked the lady for kindly allowing us to come in. She said I was fortunate to have come now because they planned on knocking the house down and rebuilding next year.

I looked up and with tear filled eyes whispered, 'Thank you, God.' I couldn't have felt more grateful in that moment.

Our next stop was Hamina, to meet my brother and sister-in-law. As we walked from the car over to the café I could see my brother walking over from the other side of the road. Excitement was bubbling within again. Here was my biological brother standing before me, who I hadn't seen for thirty years.

As we were getting ready to leave the café my sister-in-law said to me, 'Don't you want to come to our home and see the house in which you once lived?' She explained that they had purchased a neighbouring house to my biological mother's home and would gladly show me around.

Looking at our driver for approval, he nodded with a smile.

Getting out of the car at their house I saw a young, handsome man walking towards me. It was my nephew! We connected instantly and it was as though we'd always known each other.

It was now our second-to-last day in Finland and we were about to catch a train to Espoo where my older sister lived. Her husband picked us up from the train station, and as we drove to their house I felt like a kid in a candy store — I was so excited to meet her! I also met two more nephews whom I felt very drawn to.

We had a lifetime to catch up on in the five hours that we were there. Sadly, my sister informed me that she had end-stage colon cancer. The news ripped my heart to pieces. I had just reunited with her, but for how long?

A few weeks after returning to Australia I was prompted to look through old letters that I'd received from my biological mother thirty years ago. To my surprise, in one of the letters, she stated that my biological father had a son, so this meant that I had another brother!

I immediately searched for his name on Facebook and Google, finding a profile which I felt sure was him. I wrote him a private message and I awoke to a reply the following morning which sprung me out of bed like a bullet.

'Yes indeed, Liisa, we are related,' he responded. My heart was dancing.

God whispered to my soul, 'I will restore to you the years the locusts have stolen.'

Sign Language
Julia Archer

'Someone told me you know where the School for the Deaf is located?'

'Um, yes,' I said. 'We took two children from the slum playgroup there. To see if the school would accept them as students.'

'Would you take me to visit the school, before I go home to Sweden?'

'Sure. I'd love to. What about Tuesday?'

It was 1992, and Anna and I were among ten volunteer teachers at a small English conversation school in Islamabad, Pakistan. Our students were young refugee women, and it was a really happy place to work and to learn. The teachers were Christian missionaries from North America, Scandinavia and Korea.

Except for me. I was the wife of an Australian technical advisor on a UN aid project.

The other teachers teased me a bit about my Australian English. But I was more amazed that some of our students would eventually resettle in Sweden, where they would speak English with a Korean accent!

My other — unrelated — volunteer role at the time was to pick up young children from their mud brick slum community, and drive them to a weekly playgroup for children with a disability.

And so my two roles came together the day my Swedish friend Anna and I set out for the School for the Deaf. Did I actually remember the route from the day I took Imran and Fauzia for their placement tests? I hoped so!

The school came into sight just where I'd hoped it was. We parked, went in and found the principal.

Anna explained why we had come. 'I used to work with the deaf in Sweden. I would love to meet one of your classes.'

The principal was a little uncertain. This was out of the ordinary, in a culture where routine is much preferred. But Pakistani culture is also courteous and hospitable.

'I will take you to meet our senior class.'

The principal led the way up the raw concrete stairs. The building was new, and basic. But for an Islamabad government school it was pretty good. Someone in officialdom had cared about these students, I could see that.

We looked through the open door of the classroom, and the first thing that struck me as out of the ordinary was not the silence - it was the teenage girls and boys sharing a class.

Primary schools in Pakistan were coeducational. But here were teenage girls and boys in class together as if it were the most normal thing in the world.

And they were signing to each other, and the teacher.

When I had come before, there were electronic communication devices, and hearing aids. But who was going to pay for the batteries and the maintenance of those devices, I'd wondered.

Well, problem solved. Sign language had been taught, and learned, and mastered. These children had reached the senior level of high school.

Wow.

The three of us walked in, and heads turned. Visitors! One a tall blonde woman with bright blue eyes! Now *that* doesn't happen every day!

'Hi,' Anna signed, in the sign language she learned in Sweden.

The class was electrified.

'Hi,' signed back the ones who had got their wits together (mostly girls).

Well, at that point I lost track of the conversation, but I saw the effect. If uproar can happen in almost total silence, we had uproar.

Hands were flying, Anna's and the students' (mostly the girls). As the principal and I watched on (and no doubt the principal was following the conversation) a flurry of questions was asked and answered.

Someone pointed to me and asked a question.

As far as I followed it, the answer was, 'Oh, she's only the driver. She can't even sign.'

At which point all interest in such an ignorant person was lost.

I was quite content to be on the sidelines. I was riveted by what was happening. It was clear the girls were ahead in either their skills or their ability to rise to the novel occasion. It was funny to watch a confused boy sign a question and a girl turn impatiently and sign him back an explanation.

What was the class teacher thinking? What did the principal make of this interruption to routine? I won't ever know. But I do remember very clearly what I thought as I stood there watching.

Those children had worked and struggled and failed and tried again over several years, to master a skill not much valued in wider Pakistani society.

When I had come before, and seen the electronic aids on the desks, I had asked about sign language, and been told off.

'You think because we are a Third World country that's good enough for us! You wouldn't accept it for your own deaf people!'

Well, yes we do. As I write this story, I think of how signing has been valued in Australia in this year of multiple disasters. Validated at the highest level as the skilful Auslan interpreters stand beside premiers, fire and police chiefs, and state and federal medical officers, and spread the message of the day. Sometimes I've missed what the premier or police chief said, I was so busy watching the Auslan interpreter!

As I watched those teens that day, interacting with Anna, I felt quite emotional.

They came from an Urdu-speaking community. Even their parents probably didn't speak English, Anna's second (audible) language. Anna couldn't speak Urdu, either.

But she could come from the other side of the world and walk into their classroom and hold a rapid-fire conversation with them.

I thought of how they had persevered and learned this language, and maybe they wondered if it had any use outside their little school community on the outskirts of Islamabad. If all their effort meant anything, really.

And Anna had told them — Yes! It does mean something beyond this school. You are part of a worldwide community who sign, who speak across the barriers of national languages.

She had validated their struggle, their achievement.

Yes, I felt a bit emotional.

I wondered if she realised what she had done.

The morning classes ended, students poured down the stairwell, other classes were asking, 'Who are the visitors?' Hands were flying. Question. Answer. More questions.

They didn't want to let Anna go. We all milled about in the foyer until the principal thanked us for coming, and we walked back to the car.

I tried to share with Anna what I thought she'd done for those teenagers. I'd like to think she got it, but maybe my communication skills weren't up to the task.

An Imperfect Mum
Karen Curran

O-L-N-Y... Jenni frowned as she slowly printed the letters.

'It's spelled this way, Sweetie,' I said. I wrote *O-N-L-Y*, then pointed to a blank space on her sheet of paper. 'Why don't you practice?'

After copying the word several times, Jenni turned the paper over and tried again.

O-L-N-Y.

When I pointed out her error, Jenni burst into tears. I took a deep breath and closed my eyes as her crying turned to screaming.

ONLY was the last in a string of words I had been trying to help my daughter spell. She had trouble with all of them: too few letters, too many letters, letters in the wrong place. With this final word, she snapped — and so did I, moving to distance myself.

It's not supposed to be like this, I thought as I walked rapidly toward my bedroom. *I can't help her.*

My eight-year-old son, Chris, followed me down the hall and what he said stopped me in my tracks.

'It's okay, Mummy. We love you. You don't have to be perfect.'

Speechless, I cried as my son hugged me. I knew Chris was right. It was not the first time he had amazed me with his ability to sort through matters of the heart and mind.

As I relaxed in my room, my mind slowly cleared. I was upset because I couldn't help my six-year-old learn to spell. But my son saw more deeply: he saw my despair at not being a perfect mother. Apparently, my long battle with perfectionism was not over.

God, forgive me.

I was humbled to know that my son was an observer of my inner struggle, and frightened to consider the impact my striving had on my children. Instead of accepting myself as God created me, I was berating myself for my shortcomings. How would my children ever learn to trust God with such an example?

Help me, Lord, to be content with doing the best I can. Help me to lean on you. Help me entrust to you my children and my parenting abilities.

My son and daughter gave me a glimpse of who I really was and the image was not flattering. As I talked with God in the days that followed, he reminded me that only he is perfect. God filled my heart with a passion to love and parent my children well, but didn't intend for me to do it on my own. Even though he has told me numerous times to give my burden of perfectionism to him, it was only when my children became involved that I finally saw my need to look to God.

I don't like to see my imperfections. But I love my children, and I love being their mother. What's more, I love God and I want my life to bring glory to him. Maybe one way to do that is to simply find joy in letting God work through an imperfect mum.

Snakes, Ladders and Green Carpets
Anusha Atukorala

Moving house is one of life's most stressful events. But twenty years ago, when looking for our first home in Adelaide, God led us to a cosy little nest. It was like catching a plump trout the moment we threw a fishing tackle in the water.

During the first fifteen years we lived there, whenever my husband suggested a move, I'd shake my head. *Not yet.* The thing is, I would have liked to live there forever.

But as the years sped by, our needs altered. Taking care of the spacious garden became an unwelcome chore. We grew older and discovered that we preferred a house on flat ground. What I had loved most about our home was that with magnificent views, a large yard and beauty surrounding us, it was easy to connect with God. Would we ever find another home where his presence was palpable?

What if we found a house that was right for us but with no magic in it? What then?

Once we made the decision to sell our home, there was no time to be lost. I spent all my waking hours decluttering, cleaning, tidying, and paying frequent visits to the Salvos to donate books, clothes and all kinds of paraphernalia. My head was in a constant whirl and my body was perpetually fatigued. It felt too hard, but like soldiers preparing for battle, we had to keep going, placing one foot in front of the other. At last, after three months of feverish activity, we were ready.

I thought that the hardest part was over. *How little I knew!*

At first, all went according to plan. Our initial housing inspection brought in twenty-two groups of people, and the agent was buoyant. He promptly fixed an extra inspection for the next week … on my birthday at that. I had a good feeling about it and I was right. That night we received an offer well above our asking price. It was all happening!

The next weekend, contract signed, my family spent an exciting day visiting twelve houses that were up for purchase. They all had their own appeal but I wasn't convinced any of them were right for us. I continued to scan the web, pressing my button of HOPE over and over again.

One evening, after looking at a particular house, I wasn't impressed.

Who would want a house with green carpets?

But then ... a moment later, I had an urgent sense that I needed to look again.

I ran to my computer, turned it on and scanned the photographs. Like the morning sun rising from behind dark clouds, truth began to dawn, setting my heart ablaze. This house contained every feature we hoped for. It was perfect, despite its green carpets — or perhaps because of them. It could be our green season — a season of growth and lush beauty. We went for the house's first inspection. As I walked through it, savouring all my eyes alighted on, a deep joy welled up within me — it was God's confirmation that *this* was the one. Yes, we had found our dream home.

Walking trails extended outside its front door, and a pretty little nature reserve was just a few minutes' walk away. Picturesque mountain views beckoned us from both the kitchen and front yard. When my husband's eyes lit up as he walked through, it was the icing on my cake. The house was walking distance from our doctor, hairdresser, dentist, shops and church. What more could we ask for? But there was one little snag. The asking price was way above what we could afford.

By the end of the next week, a new complication occurred — our buyers pulled out of their contract! *What*? Yes. Like sliding down a snake in a game of snakes and ladders, we slithered all the way down back to Square One! It was time to return to hard work, pushing our bodies well beyond their capabilities. I even fell down twice, receiving bruises, a black eye, a cut lip and a hurt knee.

What about our Dream Home? Miraculously, its selling price was brought down significantly not once but twice, until it sat squarely within our price range. Unbelievable! On Sundays, I'd drive to the little reserve next to it to pray. Every time I did, I felt a quickening within my spirit—a nudge from God that this was the home he had hand-picked for us. Loving family and friends also supported us through their faithful prayers.

The weeks went by, but not a single offer came in for our home. At the final open inspection before Christmas, we were discouraged, disillusioned and depressed. I felt I could not go one step further on this housing journey. I was just too weary.

That's when it happened.

Our agent gave us incredible news: We had an offer!

Really? Hope, like a colour-splashed rainbow, smiled across our grey skies.

It was below our price range so we held out for more. A week later, after two more open inspections, the offer was increased.

Twelve open inspections completed, one house sold. *Hooray*!

The next morning we raced to another open inspection of our Dream Home where my husband made an offer. Were we too late? It was the Christmas season and everyone was on holidays. After a nail-biting ten days, we signed a contract on our Dream Home. You'd think we could finally breathe easy. But no, like a crocodile refusing to release its prey, trouble scrunched us in its jaws again.

We paid for a building inspection of the property during the cooling off period, sure that all would be well. Unfortunately the building inspector called us to give us news we didn't want to hear — the house could have major structural issues. *Oh no!* He told us we needed a plumbing inspection completed in order to ensure there was no problem. But when we asked the agent for more time to check on the problem, he refused. In deep shock, we had no choice but to walk away from our contract.

On Monday morning after my husband left for work, I sat in our family room, tears wetting my blouse as they splashed down, unchecked. 'Lord, You convinced me that this is the home You had prepared for us. Not once but many times over. I don't understand.'

'This *is* the home I have for you, dear child. Will you trust me?'

'But God … it can never be!' I cried. 'We've reached the point of no return!'

I sat there for a long time. Finally, I gave God my Dream Home. As I sat in his presence, God reminded me of the promise he'd given me the day before.

'The Lord your God will give you rest by giving you this land' (Joshua 1:13). The words seeped into my being. Like a ship that had found safe harbour, they settled within.

Twenty-four hours later, the agent called us. The owners had a plumbing inspection done. *Were we interested in seeing it?* On the 18th of January, 2018 we signed a contract on our new home. I knelt before God, my heart overflowing with gratitude, awe and praise.

We have now been in our new home for over two years. Every day I thank God for what he did. I'm still overwhelmed, not only because he brought us into our Dream Home, (perfect for us in every way), but that he also worked a series of what I believe are miracles in order to get us here. Through the journey, he taught me, moulded me, transformed me. He showed me who he is, a God who orders our steps, who cares for us and for whom nothing is impossible.

I type these words from my little den — the study cum prayer room that God provided for me in our new home. I hadn't even asked him for one. It was his bonus gift. Oh, and by the way, as for beauty, God's presence and that sense of magic I longed for … nooks and crannies filled with enchantment sing out to me all day long.

I am content.

Snakes, Ladders and Green Carpets

I am home.

His Eye is on the Budgie
Lesley Beth Manuel

I was eight. My sister and I were fortunate. Our house in Balmoral, Brisbane, sported a large backyard where many cubby houses were erected from boxes, planks, old blankets and cut-up banana tree trunks. Unlike the boy next door, whose yard was manicured to within an inch of its life, we were free to dig, build and have imaginary adventures in Africa if we chose. And we had pets!

My much-loved, blue budgie had everything he needed. Occasionally, when his wings were clipped, Winkie had free run of the lounge room.

One Friday after school, I gave Winkie his 'get-out-of-cage-free' treat.

Much to my surprise, his wings were working *very* well!

Overdue for a clipping?

Disaster!

Winkie's urge to fly was too strong and he escaped into the world of trees, open sky and suburbia. I should have closed all the doors!

Screams alerted my parents and we scrambled in pursuit. We searched backyard trees, cubby houses and the street but found nothing. Not even a discarded blue feather!

The sun was dropping over Winkie's unpredictable new world. The lengthening shadows mirrored my mothering fears. *Could he find his way home? He might be attacked by a cat!*

Dark dread settled over me.

The abandoned cage loomed larger than normal.

As was her habit, Mum came to tuck me into bed.

'Mum, ask God to bring Winkie back,' I implored.

Mum hesitated, and then prayed.

I relented to a restless sleep.

Filled with expectant searching, Saturday and Sunday came and went.

His Eye is on the Budgie

Hadn't God heard?

I lugged my heartache to Bulimba State School.

My best friend, Carol, heard the news first: 'I lost my budgie.'

With surprising urgency, she blurted back, 'What colour is he?'

'Blue,' I replied

Carol's response was totally unexpected. 'The other day, Dad caught a blue budgie in our back yard.'

Excitement bubbled. 'What? Could it be Winkie?'

'You can come and see,' Carol said with a smile.

With hope hanging over me, the day dragged.

Winkie's cage perched optimistically next to me as Dad drove the two kilometres to my friend's house. Carol's parents took us to their terraced garden where their recently found budgie had been prevented from further independence. There he was, perched sheepishly in a foreign cage: 'Winkie!'

I was elated. God cleverly arranged Winkie's return — even if it had taken two days.

Maybe God knew Winkie needed a two-day sightseeing vacation!

Years later, my mother shared that she had worried what it would do to my faith if Winkie hadn't come back. She said that after the miraculous way Winkie was returned, I believed God could do anything. Now, whenever I see a sparrow, I recall Ethel Waters singing *His Eye is on the Sparrow*, and I am reminded of Winkie, and the fact that God will always watch over me — no matter how far I fly.

A Letter to You

Beverly Sweeney

I apologise for not having a name for You when I was younger, but perhaps that's okay. Now, many decades later, I think that to name You is sometimes to commit You to a tiny box of people's expectations and fears.

But I digress.

In the past, I did not give You much thought, other than that many people seemed to need You, possibly as a crutch. And that was fine with me. (Oh, the precociousness of youth!). It crossed my mind, however, that one day I too may need a crutch.

Then, in my late forties, my world collapsed. Flashbacks came out of the blue — completely repressed memories erupted: me as a tiny child; him a disturbed young man. Either these memories were grounds for madness, or they were true. If true, however, how could it be? I had no normal recollection of them. I began to question my sanity.

My body would replay the trauma of each memory, leaving me curled in terror and exhaustion for hours. Frequently over the next year I hovered on the precipice of a complete breakdown. Each time, however, something dragged me back, to rest and recover, ready to deal with the next explosion. I gave that something a name: 'The Process.' There was obviously some kind of protective mechanism at work.

But I still lived in a constant state of terror, never knowing what was to come next.

One day a counsellor suggested, 'Next time you feel a memory emerging, sit up and face it. Try to welcome the fear. It's really just a part of you.'

So I did. I sat in a chair and tried to open my heart to the fear instead of dreading it as I had always done. And You embraced me like a long lost child. A great peace filled my body and my mind. I felt I was sitting in a beam of light and I knew beyond a doubt that You were that beam of light and I finally knew Your name.

You stayed with me, and over eighteen months drew me towards one of Your homes. You sent me missives in dreams, guided my hand as I wrote poetry. Finally, in a workshop for survivors, You sent me a message through a Bible reading:

When thou passest through the waters I will be with thee; and through the rivers, they shall not overflow thee: when thou walkest through the fire, thou shalt not be burned; neither shall the flame kindle upon thee (Isaiah 43:2).

I felt called to go to Christ's Mass.

On Christmas Eve, I accompanied my neighbours to our little local Catholic Church. As we stood for the entrance hymn and the priest proceeded towards the altar, my body began to tremble uncontrollably and tears erupted in my eyes.

I knew You had shepherded me home.

God's Love in the Home

Colleen Russell

When I round the bend in the road, I enter a new world — a place of peace, where the home light always glows.

The house smiles at me. It's like a child's illustration — a door with windows on either side with green shutters, and in winter, a wisp of chimney smoke slowly escaping to the heavens.

There's a picket fence and a sandstone path leading to the tiled verandah, with jasmine entwined on the verandah posts — its fragrance entrancing the senses. Hanging baskets sway carelessly in the breeze, pendant with the multi-colours of seasonal flowers.

A laneway at the side of the house leads to a large camellia tree covered with white flowers, standing like a sentinel, forever on guard, amid the rich smell of earth and freshly mown grass.

The gate rasps as it opens, reminding me that the hinges need oiling. Buddy beats me to the front door, his tail wagging a greeting, his long tongue lolling with a perpetual grin, waiting to be welcomed home.

He doesn't realise that there is no one waiting.

But my mother stands at the door, smiling. Can't you see her? Buddy can. She's waiting for us, will always be waiting for us.

Mum despaired when she first saw the house, a rental place, run down and neglected by a series of careless tenants. Over time we gave it our attention, and years later, the place was offered for sale. The purchase was concluded within fifteen minutes, and the house belonged to us, at last.

My sister and I thrived in our shared room, where dust motes tumbled in the light rays from the tall window.

Our parents' bedroom looked out across the valley to the blue of the sea, where white horses galloped across the peaks of the waves. On the edge of the valley stood the two-storied schoolhouse we attended each day and where my mother had taught in an earlier time.

I am fair with blue eyes, but my sister was the opposite — dark, with eyes of melted chocolate. The kitchen was her castle. She loved to cook and the kitchen garden flourished under her green thumb.

Every room bore my mother's touch — vases of perfumed flowers, the interior cool during the heat of summer, warm and sheltering from the winter winds off the ocean. Our home was full of God's love.

At mealtimes we sang grace: *All Things Bright and Beautiful.* Our lives were blessed.

Now, all are gone, and I am the only one left to remember the love.

My bags stand in the hallway, packed with my dreams. I'm not looking back. I have my memories to cherish, forever.

The For Sale sign claps in the breeze; on the kitchen counter is a tall vase of Mum's roses, now brown and withered.

Buddy looks up at me expectantly.

'Yes, Bud. It's just you and me now.'

That Wonderful Peace

Jeanette Grant-Thomson

Papua New Guinea, 1972. The scorching Rabaul sunshine slanted through the louvres in my friend Robyn's flat. I was holidaying there after teaching a year in New Ireland, a separate island in this equatorial country. I'd flown over for a break.

'I'm going to look in the Chinese shops and then walk around near the harbour,' I told Robyn as she left for work. I was excited. Rabaul, in those days, was stunningly beautiful.

I combed my hair, ready to go.

Suddenly, a tangible peace cloaked me with gentle strength.

I paused to enjoy it. The heavy tropical air was moist and hot, but I no longer noticed it pressing on my skin. All I could feel was wonderful peace — God's presence.

This must be the peace that passes all understanding the Bible mentions.

I felt so calm. So strong.

If I always felt like this, I could do anything and cope with anything at all.

My thoughts were interrupted by the screech of tyres in the driveway. Footsteps clattered up the steps. My brother-in-law's black curly hair and worried face appeared at the door.

'John!' I exclaimed. 'I thought you and Wendy were in Tufabi.' (Tufabi is on a separate large island.)

'Your sister's in hospital...' John's voice broke. 'She's very sick ... might die ... sent here as a medical emergency... life-threatening infection...'

Wendy... my strong, calm, sister with the long brown hair... die? But she was so young and healthy...

Yet all through those terrible words, I remained bathed in supernatural peace. For a moment my mind swam with shock and horror, but I felt no fear — only normal concern.

'Pick you up in ten minutes,' John said before driving off.

I hurried to my room and sank to my knees. Weeping, but cocooned in peace, I asked, 'Father, will she... die?'

The peace grew stronger. A gentle presence like a fine silk shawl rested over me.

Clear words formed in my mind. *She will not die.*

Relief flooded me. Quickly I packed things Wendy might need and was ready when John returned. We drove straight to the hospital.

Wendy's ward seemed strangely dim.

Was it poorly lit? Or dimmed only by my emotions?

Wendy lay there, her face a yellowish-green against the white pillowcase. Dark-skinned nurses slipped silently around her, adjusting her drip, writing on her chart.

I talked to her and prayed for her, then left quietly. All the time I felt a strong Presence holding me up, and an amazing peace sustaining me.

With good medical help and visits from a super-calm sister, Wendy gradually recovered and, after a few weeks, was back in Tufabi.

I have always been thankful for that supernatural peace that enabled me to do all I had to do — calmly, without my own fear affecting Wendy. I had strong, quiet faith to pray for her healing. It was a little miracle, too, that after teaching all year on New Ireland I happened to be in Rabaul for Wendy's crisis.

The Way to Remember
Jennie Del Mastro

We sat on the deck with cups of tea and watched the kids swinging. The memorial service was over and my sister and her daughter were on the plane back to WA. The house already seemed very quiet.

'When should the kids be back at school?' asked Mum.

'Probably next Monday,' I said.

'You should go, too, honey.'

'Mum…'

'I'll be fine.'

But it was only a few weeks since she'd stepped through the doorway of this house, knowing Dad would never live here again. She couldn't stay here alone — not yet.

'I'll be fine,' she repeated. 'I need to be alone, to process this.'

The first night back home, I couldn't sleep. I pushed away thoughts of Dad, who was safe and well now but had suffered so much as the mesothelioma destroyed him. I couldn't fathom the idea that he was gone, and I didn't try yet. Instead, I stared into the darkness and thought of Mum.

I hated that I'd left her. How would she be able to live there by herself? How could she even look at the walls that Dad had painted, or open doors that he'd sanded and polished? How could she sleep in their bed alone?

'God, I don't know what to do!'

I know the plans I have for you… plans to prosper you and not to harm you… plans to give you a hope and a future.

My spinning thoughts grew still. The verse seemed to come randomly to my mind, but I knew that didn't happen. God had good plans for Mum's future, however impossible that seemed. He was telling me, and I had to tell her.

I repeated the verse to myself, impressing it on my mind. I would ring Mum first thing.

Next morning when I woke, I'd forgotten it ever happened. I hadn't forgotten Mum, though.

'Maybe we should go back to Melbourne this weekend,' I said to my husband.

'Definitely,' he said.

Mum's house was filled with cards and the scent of lilies. She told me about the new routines, the people who visited, how her freezer was full of dinners, and how she hated dead flowers. Sometimes she stopped talking and cried, and I hugged her.

My heart ached for her. She hadn't only lost Dad, but twenty or thirty more happy years they could have shared. It was too deep a wound to survive. How could she face the future? What could I do?

'I listened to the last church service podcast,' Mum said, blowing her nose. 'They spoke about that verse: *I know the plans I have for you.*'

'What? They did?' The memory rushed back. I was dumbfounded. Maybe God didn't expect me to be a pillar of strength after all.

'Honey, thank you for everything you do,' Mum said. 'But don't forget he was your father, not just my husband.'

This time I cried, and she hugged me.

With You
Lisa Birch

The car suddenly swerved one way, then another. The pop music we had been singing along to was playing like an eerie soundtrack to a movie it didn't belong in. Then the car started to roll and everything went black.

When I came to, the music had stopped and we were upside down, held in place by our seatbelts. I touched the roof with my fingers. A red mark, still wet, contrasted with the tan interior. I touched my head. The red mark on the roof was blood, and it belonged to me.

I looked over at my friend and we silently scrambled out of the wreckage together evading the glass shards around us. Though our trip had been on a Saturday afternoon, we barely saw any cars until the accident had happened. Suddenly half a dozen were parked along the highway, one person calling an ambulance, another with the biggest first aid kit in the world.

The emergency services arrived. I complained about my sore neck and before I knew it I was in a neck-brace in the back of an ambulance racing towards the nearest hospital. It felt wrong that I was in an ambulance, instead of still in the warm car on the long-planned road trip. It suddenly dawned on me: we're not going to make it to the conference.

In my hometown there were lots of churches but for whatever reason I felt closest to Christian culture when I was surrounded by hundreds of strangers who had the same faith. The same people who wanted to spend three days and nights 'getting equipped' the way I did. The last few years I had attended events like this had brought upon radical change in my life and I wanted more of the same. Something about a huge conference or concert gave me the special nudge I needed to keep going. God felt closer to me in those places.

The thought of missing the conference was soon swept away by another thought. This accident was not a surprise. For weeks now I'd been waking at 3 am, worrying about the road trip. Neither of us were experienced in long distance driving and I had always been a worrier. I thought about all of the ways around it and it seemed there were none except just take the chance and drive. And anyway, surely God wanted me to go to this conference, right?

Guilt had overtaken me by the time I'd been admitted to hospital. I hadn't listened to God and look where it landed me: a little hospital in the middle of Woop Woop, getting anti-nausea injections in my backside.

The wannabe-youth pastor in me spent the night in a hospital bed thinking about how this could all be turned into an object lesson. I could say things like, 'I didn't listen to God calling me away from something and look where I landed. Upside down in a car!' I knew my youth group kids at home would eat it up and judging by the messed up state of my hands, I'd have some epic battle scars to show them. Fantasising about my life as a preacher-girl got me through the long evening where I was immobile and scared.

When I arrived home the next day my brothers had thrown me a welcome home party complete with handmade cards, a mud cake, and decorations. They might have been the best brothers a girl could wish for but I was just too unwell to celebrate my homecoming. After a week I had my stitches taken out and after two weeks I was able to open and close my hands, even though they were banged up with their gnarly scars.

After a month I moved out of home and set up a pin board with my 'get well soon' cards on it to remind me of everyone. I had two lives: a life in the city where I went to Bible college, and a life back at home with my parents and my brothers. I had thought that Bible college would be like being at that conference I had missed out on, but there was no hype involved, just hard work and deep insta-friendships.

At college I read books about trauma and did a course in counselling, hoping to find some answers to the intrusive thoughts. My thoughts were a little mixed up with real life. It seemed every few months someone I knew was impacted by road trauma.

'Everyone I know seems to be getting into accidents,' I said after class one day to one of the guys in my counselling class. 'It's like I'm jinxed.'

'If you keep saying that you'll speak it into being,' he warned. It added to my worries. Was I causing this somehow? No one around me was able to see that the connections between my community and road trauma were triggering anxiety I didn't know I had. I started reading the Scriptures looking for historical figures who hadn't listened to God.

'Maybe I'm like Jacob, who wrestled with God? Because I wouldn't listen to him?'

'It doesn't work like that,' a friend told me, his voice quite firm. 'That's not even the way the story goes.' I didn't listen. For a few months I played that role in my mind: the woman who God himself spoke to and she didn't listen.

'Maybe these scars are to remind me that I can't do it on my own. Like, I need God's help and stuff?' I mused to a college friend.

'What scars? Are they on your legs or something?' I vaguely pointed at my slightly mangled hands, my tiny ear scar. Slightly miffed that she hadn't got to the heart of the question I quickly changed the topic.

The guilt of not listening, of not being a faithful servant, consumed me. I wanted to have spiritual stories, real pain of knowing myself and God. Something to tell people, to make them feel something, to tell them 'I've suffered too,' even though in our counselling class we were reminded in every lecture that we don't need to go through deep pain to help others through their own.

In the face of the constant questioning I had already been given an answer. It was annoyingly right up there on the pin up board inside a card.

'Just remember, God is always with you.'

My brother had written it inside the card he made the night of my homecoming party and I had dismissed it as a placation rather than something meaningful.

God was never punishing me for a decision I made. Before it happened, I may have thought the accident was a slight possibility, and I knew that those early morning worry sessions weren't God trying to help me solve a problem. It was a conversation, not a strategising session. Whether I wanted to admit it or not, God had been with me, every step of the way, whether I was saved by a seatbelt or whether I was trying to process news stories of road trauma. He was always there. Conference or no conference, there wasn't anywhere I could escape his presence.

In God's Garden
Heather Gray

We were excited to be visiting our projects in the Philippines again. The night before we left, we called in to our son Rob's, to say goodbye. Rob's daughter, Willow, was seven and half months old. She had just started saying 'Mum-mum… Dad-dad…' and 'Bub-bub…' Rob was so pleased she had called him 'Dad'. Willow babbled away as she sat bouncing on my knee. Rob took her, changed her nappy then held her up, a smile of pride lighting his face. We finally said goodbye and left to prepare for our journey the next day.

We had good flights to Manila and Cebu, then headed for the island of Boracay on a light aircraft to join friends for a few days. The last part of our journey to the island was on an outrigger boat. It was a beautiful day and soon we were swimming in the crystal blue waters. Next day, we visited another island. We headed to a cave where we dived and swam. Lunch awaited us on yet another island. Before us was an eye-catching array of fish and we each chose one to be cooked.

A few days later we went to San Carlos where we were to hand over two vehicles and open the first stage of the Community and Worship Centre on Sunday. Sunday also happened to be my birthday.

In the early hours of Sunday morning the phone rang. One of the young people staying with us answered. She came and woke us, saying, 'It is a call from Australia.'

Not realising the time, I replied, 'It's probably a call from the family to wish me a happy birthday.' I took the phone.

'Mum…' It was the voice of our daughter. 'Willow's dead…'

'What!' I exclaimed.

By this time Bob was awake. 'What is it?' he asked.

'Willow's dead.'

We couldn't believe what we were hearing.

Next, our other son, Darren, rang from the hospital. He was there with his brother, Rob, and Karly, Willow's mother, and some other family members. It seemed Rob had woken to check on Willow and found she wasn't breathing. The ambulance came, but all attempts to revive her failed.

Somehow we got through the rest of the night, overcome with grief, and unable to go back to sleep.

When I arose, I went out and stood beside a nearby stream. The sun was just beginning to colour the morning sky. As I stood there, my heart was filled with grief — not only for the loss of our precious granddaughter, but also for our son and daughter-in-law and the suffering for them in the loss of their first child. Gazing at that beautiful sunrise, I sensed God's promise to me that Willow was safe in his heavenly garden.

Part of me went to Heaven that day. Thirteen years have passed, but not a day goes by when I do not think of Willow. I envisage her playing in that garden, knowing that one day we will see her again.

Only a Male
R.J. Rodda

In grade three, my class pet was a red-eyed, white-haired guinea pig. I would crouch down to watch her snuffle around her cage, sniff at the wood shavings and eat her pellets. Then one day she did something even more fascinating. She gave birth to babies.

This gave me an idea. My birthday was approaching and of course I wanted my own guinea pig and not just any guinea pig but one that was exactly like the one at school. Red-eyed, white haired and a mother with babies.

On hearing my request, my fair-haired mother drew in a breath and declared, 'No babies. But possibly one male guinea pig. I'll talk to Dad about it.'

Dad agreed with Mum, but the desire I had for baby guinea pigs would not go away. There was only one thing to do. Pray. God had answered my prayer for a cat. Couldn't he answer my prayer for baby guinea pigs too? I clasped my hands together and asked him, night after night.

Meanwhile Mum went to the pet shop and ordered a white male guinea pig with red eyes.

On the day of my birthday, I got him and named him Precious. He was very cute but inwardly I was a bit disappointed. I'd prayed for baby guinea pigs. Why hadn't God answered?

Still, I enjoyed having Precious. I would imitate his squeaks and cuddle him. During the day, I would lie outside on the lawn next to his cage, watching him eat the grass. During the cooler nights, he was moved onto the top of a low cupboard in our playroom and I would talk to him there.

One evening as we were all dashing about to leave the house for a meeting, Mum ducked into the playroom for something. 'Rebekah… Rebekah!' she shrieked.

I came running into the dimly lit playroom. Mum cried out, 'Precious is giving birth. She's just had one baby.'

Only a Male

To my amazement, I got to see one cute little dark orange fluff and another black and white one enter the world.

We exclaimed over them for quite some time. Then Mum shook her head in bewilderment. 'I just don't understand. I asked the pet shop, quite clearly, for a male guinea pig. How could they give me a pregnant female?'

I knew why, because I had prayed and God loved me enough to give me the desire of my childish heart.

Pterodactyl

Grant Lock

A grimy garden glove bangs on the window of my home office. 'Come quickly Grant!'

I look up. Janna is shouting, 'It moved! It moved!'

'What moved?'

'The oily rag! Come on! We have to save it!'

I stumble out to the garden. Who … saves oily rags?

Janna is peering down into an old, white pipe.

When the former owners planted a young tree, they buried a short length of PVC pipe, upright, into the ground. They filled the pipe with water and it seeped down into the roots of the young tree. It worked. The tree is now tall and green.

'Grant. I was cleaning up, and I looked down this pipe… there's an old oily rag down there!'

Now, my wife likes to clean things up properly. Leaves and dead twigs don't stand a chance. And neither does a dirty old rag. It doesn't matter if it is hidden, half a metre down an unused pipe. It just shouldn't be there. It makes the place untidy.

She's shaking. 'I pushed this stick down to get it out.'

'And …?'

'It moved! And then it hissed.'

My body stiffens.

'No no! It's not a snake Grant. It's … it's our Bluetongue!'

Now she is making sense. We are both very fond of our Bluetongue lizard. He pokes around the garden. We talk to him a bit, and then he wriggles off under the bushes.

'Grant! We have to do something! He could be nearly dead!'

The pipe extends twenty centimetres above ground level. 'I don't know how he climbed up into it, or why. But one thing is certain: he could never get out. Who knows how long he has been trying to scratch his way up that slippery pipe? He had the run of the garden. Now he is trapped.

Pterodactyl

To that Bluetongue, the barbecue tongs must have looked like the savage jaws of some ancient Pterodactyl. He didn't know it was to be his saviour. He raised his head. He hissed, and fought.

But the tongs kept coming.

We can be like that... trapped in a human-made hole. Scratching. Scratching, at the dark, slippery sides of life. God reaches down to restore us. We may hiss, and fight. But he keeps on coming. He lifts us out. He feeds us. He refreshes us.

Our Bluetongue planted his front feet in a saucer of water, and lapped and licked. He nibbled at some small pieces of mince-meat. Then he crawled away into the Agapanthus. Janna and I looked at each other and smiled, and then we started to laugh. We felt so good. It gave us so much pleasure to save our 'oily-rag' lizard.

Somehow, in that moment, we experienced a morsel of God's great pleasure and joy when he lifts his much-loved mortals out of dark, slippery places.

After all, it was for us, that with joy, he endured the tongs of death, to restore us to the run of the garden.

Our Story during the Pandemic
Cris Yu

In Mathew 19:14 Jesus says, 'Let the children come to me. Don't stop them! For the kingdom of Heaven belongs to those who are like these children.' I actually heard teaching on this verse many times but I never reached such a vivid understanding on the meaning as I did during the COVID pandemic while I was literally stuck with two children in a house for months.

It could be scary trying to sort things out between the two of them. One is a pre-teenager who's starting to build her own territory, and one is at an age that, in Chinese we say, is even irritating to the dogs and cats! And it could turn out to be a disaster if both of them felt I wasn't being fair. I often found that in the evening I was so tired I just wanted to throw myself into bed, skipping one key daily routine of reading the Bible together and praying. But, surprisingly, each time I wanted to quit, my son Adam would come to me insisting 'Mum, you said we would read the Bible every day and you also asked me to monitor you.' And I had no excuse.

Actually, I was amazed at how persistent they are to spend time with God by reading, sharing and praying. As an adult, I have to admit that I do sometimes wonder how God is going to respond to my prayers, but the children are so willing to present their wants and needs in prayer, no matter how things turn out. I used to collect their prayer points and pray on behalf of them because I was dumb enough to think that they're too young to pray. But I was proved wrong. Once I randomly took a step forward, suggesting that we all pray in turn — both of them didn't even hesitate. What impressed me more was that Geogia prayed not just for her own matters but also for others and the pandemic situation. And she actually said a prayer like this: 'God, if it pleases you, let us stay in Adelaide.' She has got the heart of praying.

Our Story during the Pandemic

Now I know why Jesus welcomed the children. We need them! At least I need them. They have been a reminder to me that though we might feel we're all alone sometimes, God reveals himself through people around us, our family, and our church family, that he is at work.

Twenty Square Centimetres of Power
Margot Ogilvie

It sits innocuously in the cup holder of my car. No-one else even knows it's there.

But I know. Because I understand the power it holds.

Before I got it, I was a homebody, a recluse, a stuttering introvert who avoided social interaction. I hated making phone calls. I avoided leaving the house too often. I got to church late and left quickly after the final 'Amen.'

As a mum, I'd readily spoken to my children, or about them, or for them, even to strangers. But when they grew up and didn't need me to speak for them anymore, I realised how much I preferred staying home, reclusing.

But God had other ideas! He knew it wasn't healthy for me — physically, mentally, or emotionally — to stay home alone all the time.

That's where the nametag comes in. When it's not sitting in the cup-holder of my car, its pinned to my shirt, transforming me into the highlight of people's days. With the badge firmly in place, I knock on the doors of elderly strangers and greet them cheerily. As I do whatever's needed to help them continue living at home, I chat away about anything and everything. Sometimes I'm the only person they see from one week to the next. I am their ray of sunshine, their connection to the outside world, a high point in their week.

I'm no longer a timid mouse. The nametag turns me into someone strong, confident, outgoing and bold. Someone totally different from the wallflower-in-a-crowd I used to be.

There's more on the nametag than just my name. It bears the logo of the company I work for. When I greet, with confidence and joy, the stranger who answers my knock on their door, I'm not doing it in my own strength. I'm doing it as a representative of my employer. Being the best me I can be is good for the company that pays me.

The badge also displays my title, my role. That title determines my actions. I take people shopping, but I don't spend their money for them, or advise them on financial issues. I rub moisturizer into well-worn feet, but I can't prescribe ointments or dress wounds. I'm not a nurse or a lawyer, an accountant or a priest. I'm a Home Support Worker.

One morning as I put on the badge, God spoke. In a still, small voice he said, 'You wear another badge every day.'

'What do you mean?' I replied.

'Every moment of every day, you represent me. You wear my badge.'

His badge has the logo 'Kingdom of Heaven' on it. It proves God himself, Creator of the universe, knows my name. It determines my role, not as judge or doormat, but rather as image-bearer, seed-sower, salt and light.

It makes me stand a little taller, and smile. I've got a great boss, and I've got something good to offer the world. I have a name tag from God.

Peacock
Juni Desireé Hoel

Lord, stop me.

I composed myself and quietly placed the photo of a peacock back on the sand. In a ranting frenzy, I'd been waving the picture around and yammering about how amazing the peacock was. The seven teenagers sitting around me in the shade under the gazebo must have been stunned into silence. They were probably looking at me like I was mad. Or they'd stopped paying attention ages ago and were rolling their eyes and yawning.

I'd only just met them for this Bible study on the beach for anyone who wanted to come. Now they were probably wishing they'd never come. Instead, they were probably dreaming of going back to spending their summer holidays riding their bikes. Or swimming. Or hanging out at the Maccas down the road. Or being anywhere but here. We'd been talking about God and they said they kind of believed in him but weren't sure.

'I'm getting there,' one boy said, 'but I've got too many questions.'

He came up with some wonderful questions: *Where does God get his power? Who created God? Why did God create the earth for us? How can we hear from God?*

We got talking about how we can know God is real and about different ways we can hear from him. I said it could be through anything. Through nature, the Bible, people, a conversation, a random experience. Then I spread out some pictures of nature and animals on the sand as examples of where we could see God in the world.

'I mean, look at this,' I said as I picked up the picture of a peacock with its exuberant shimmering feathers. 'How cool is God for creating such a psychedelic bird as this?'

I had no idea why out of all the pictures I singled this one out, but in that moment, it struck me just how cool the bird was. The vibrant colours, the extravagant tail, the majestic display of beauty and creativity.

'I'd never think of anything like this, but God did, and he created it. How crazy is that!'

On and on I went about the peacock. Until I realised what I was doing and I felt ridiculous. *Those poor kids*, I thought. *I'm a fool.* But when I looked up, they were nodding. I invited them to choose a picture to take home with them that could remind them of where they saw God. Quick as a flash, the boy with the questions picked up the peacock.

'Wow, why did you choose that picture?' I asked.

His brother, who was sitting next to him, started laughing. It was full-on fall-over-and-roll-on-the-sand laughter.

I looked between them bemused.

Finally, his brother sat up and said, 'It's his favourite animal.'

I laughed in disbelief. 'That's God talking to you right there,' I said to the boy with the peacock.

'I know,' he said.

We looked at each other in mirrored awe.

Where is God in my COVID-19 World?

John Duthie

I've looked for God during times when life turns upside down. Such as when a tree fell on my head and back, severing my spine at the chest level. Where are you, God?

In February 2020, the share market had a correction, followed by a crash. Every time I checked the news, it all sounded terrible, and I was getting less sleep. I was dead tired each day. Where are you, God?

The Coronavirus was spreading to aged care homes, and the health warnings suggested people aged seventy or over were at risk. I explained the dangers of the virus to my parents, including how it spreads, and how it was killing older people. They dismissed the warnings and said that they would eventually die from something. Where are you, God?

The media were suggesting that the health system would be overloaded, and doctors would have to make difficult decisions. Who would they choose to die? The people would include those with underlying health conditions. A few of my friends were susceptible, and I had paraplegia and wasn't sure if I would be provided with a ventilator. Where are you, God?

The principal weapon against the virus was isolation. I liked having people over to my home, as invites to homes were seldom forthcoming. Either their homes weren't wheelchair accessible, or they had no idea what was required. The isolation phase worried me, and I relied upon many people to help me around the home. Where are you, God?

The next disconcerting piece of news related to the levels of unemployment and businesses that were failing. Economic downturns historically affected young people harder, and my children were in their early twenties. I had two investment properties, and the property manager advised one of the tenants had decided to leave early. Where are you, God?

There were thirty other worries of mine relating to the Coronavirus, and many times I asked the same question. Where are you, God? Hindsight is always an advantage. I had a firm conviction for selling many shares, and it occurred before the correction was a crash. And then another feeling to buy back in, just after the markets started their significant rise. Our state and federal governments were making changes to help prevent the spread of the virus, as well as providing economic support. My parents didn't catch the virus, and I enjoyed the isolation. No one I knew with underlying health conditions required a ventilator. My children were busy with work and study, and a new tenant arrived.

The world faces many challenges, but a crisis, once again, taught me the same lesson. Put your faith in God. There are many worries that your actions will not change. Let God turn your big problems into less troubling concerns. God wants us to take action and do what we can and turn the rest over to God.

Jerusalem, in Egypt

Elizabeth Tobal

I've been gone for a fair while from home and loved ones.

Two and a half years earlier, I had married someone who seemed so exotic and fascinating, and we were now visiting his homeland: Egypt. Welcomed unconditionally by his warm family — even though I suppose I could have been regarded as an 'infidel' foreigner, the blue-eyed woman who didn't fit in or look the same — it had been a pleasure to get to know their town, Dammietta, and meet many of the relatives. They were simple folk who absolutely adored our little one-year-old son, calling him El Iskander (their version of Alexander!).

Could it be true, that I was actually on the very soil of the ancient Pharaohs? I had visited the Sphinx and the Pyramid of Giza — fantasy places since I was a young girl, poring over family encyclopaedias to 'discover the world beyond'. I remember many times copying my beloved older brother's painting style to bring to life maps, and scenes of daily life, never imagining that one day I would see them for myself. Egypt was always a fascination to me.

But I missed my family, especially my mother, Pearl, immensely. Just before we had flown off on our journey to Egypt, a film called 'Not Without My Daughter' was showing in the cinemas. It portrayed the struggle of a foreign-born woman attempting to flee the confines of Iran with her young child. So many people had mentioned it to me before I departed Australia: Was I concerned? What if it was like that in Egypt? What would I do if I was to become thus trapped? One dear friend even enquired if I had made a will! I tried to ignore all the well-meaning advice.

Mum and I had exchanged a few postcards during my time away — just normal home stuff; who was doing what, etc. I assured her that all was well, that we were perfectly safe and happy.

Strangely, at one time, the old hymn 'Jerusalem' had come into my mind. I remember clearly hearing the words over and over again, mulling over them and marvelling at the beauty of the song. I had heard it before, of course, but don't recall having sung it myself as we were not particularly 'churchy' people (I wasn't even baptised then).

I could not believe it when, soon after, Mum's latest missive arrived in which she described how she had been singing 'Jerusalem' out of the blue. I teed up the dates and realised it had been over *the same couple of days* that we had both been singing that hymn! I will never believe that wasn't a true spiritual message to us both, about goodness and love.

At the age of forty-three I was baptised.

At the age of fifty-four, 'Jerusalem' was played with love at Mum's funeral.

That song will forever remind me of Egypt, and Pearl.

That Question
Anna Kosmanovski

I was a university student with my head in the clouds and my hands on a duster — well, on this day, anyway.

Customers were rare so I had a lot of time to myself as I ambled the warehouse floor in the bedding shop I worked at casually.

Cleaning displays and fluffing throw cushions was on the cards today, along with my wandering thoughts.

Today I was thinking about death and the meaning of life. An avalanche of questions was snowing me down, and I was looking out for a silver bullet answer.

A thought entered my head to pray something I'd heard before, somewhere, probably from a movie.

'God, if you're real I need a sign.'

I threw the question out there, to the swirling of dust and background radio of the large shop, daring myself to hope for certainty, before returning to the swirl of questions inside.

I was actively researching religions for the one which was real, if any actually were.

More than a decade earlier, when I was thirteen, I had experienced God. Became a Christian. But now that road was so far back, I wasn't sure it even existed.

The child me had faith, but the adult me was studying journalism, knew how to research, and had access to Google late into the night...

But this assignment was worse than any university essay I'd had to write. At night, I'd think of death, eternity, death again — my heart beating so fast, as if it would launch straight out of me.

The next day brought unexpected news. I found out my cousin had been seriously injured in a terrible accident. He had emergency heart surgery and the doctors now waited to see what his recovery would be like. If he even recovered.

That Question

As soon as I heard the news, my reaction surprised me, and perhaps my family. Faith, even peacefulness, came to meet me. Somehow I just knew — God was real.

I began to see, too, that the deep answers I wanted were not found in my intellectual research. My truth was found only by faith, and pressing into the words I read that day: 'Now faith is being sure of what we hope for and certain of what we do not see' (Hebrews 11:1).

My cousin was okay — and now I was, too.

As my faith journey began again, I sensed that there were still seeds within me, buried long ago.

I was baptised, started going to church and began using my writing gift for him. Before that, my writing was cynical, but even that began to change: it's definitely more hopeful in tone now than it was before.

I can also tell you that I believe God is real. He answered my question in many ways, and still does.

And I can sleep at night now without fear of my beating heart catapulting away — unless, of course, I've indulged in too many coffees.

Promised Rescue
Emma Taylor

I sit on my bed by the window, my Bible on my lap. It's 6 pm. Peaceful. Mum's cooking. Dad's at work. So there are no arguments. No tense silences. No sunglasses to hide swollen eyes. No chance that an innocent question will shatter the peace. No phone calls drawing them out into the night to confront bad things.

A year earlier, at a Bible study for teenage girls, I had heard that God would forgive us for all the bad things we'd done if we asked Jesus to come into our life. Furthermore, this would enable us to live in right relationship with God.

'Everyone close your eyes and bow your head,' said the teacher. 'If you want to receive Jesus into your life, raise your hand.'

I raised my hand.

'Now pray after me...'

I did.

Becoming a Christian was a logical decision. But after I had apparently invited Jesus into my life, everything still seemed the same: my classmates and I were still sitting cross-legged on the concrete floor, the bell still rang and I felt exactly the same on the inside. So, I put up my hand the following week at Bible study, just in case God hadn't seen me the first-time.

I also started doing the things that Christians do: I read my Bible and prayed daily. Although I prayed that the bad things would stop, I mostly just talked to God about those bad things because my parents were preoccupied with their own problems, my sister was too young to understand, and the topic of family troubles taboo in school.

Today, my Bible reading is from Psalm 91. I read the entire song to the last stanza: *'Because he loves me,' says the Lord, 'I will rescue him. I will protect him, for he acknowledges my name. He will call upon me, and I will answer him; I will be with him in trouble, I will deliver him and honour him. With long life will I satisfy him and show him my salvation.'*

I read these words and look out the window to the valley below, clothed in deep green, an occasional wisp of smoke rising into a vast expanse of sky that's turning gold, crimson, and purple; and I whisper, 'Thank you, God for this beautiful sunset.'

Then, God replies. His inaudible-voice-presence opens my mind and he repeats the words of that last stanza, but personalises it for me:

'Because she loves me,' says the Lord, 'I will rescue her. I will protect her, for she acknowledges my name. She will call upon me, and I will answer her; I will be with her in trouble, I will deliver her and honour her. With long life will I satisfy her and show her my salvation.'

This changes everything. God sees and speaks today with compassion, even to me. Outwardly, nothing seems to change, but as the years roll on he stills my fears, heals my wounds, and grants me a home with peace, music and beautiful sunsets.

A Leap of Faith

M. J. Saladine

Sarah sat on her bed, phone in hand, nodding her head to the beat of the song playing through her headphones.

Was that a tap at the door?

She slipped off one headphone and tilted her head to listen. Nothing. She adjusted her headphones and continued to enjoy her song. A second later, the door creaked open and Dad appeared. Sarah paused her music.

'Hey, I just wanted to check in on you,' Dad said with a warm smile.

Sarah turned off her phone and placed her things down. 'I'm fine,' she replied bluntly.

'You sure?' he asked.

'Yeah, I'm all good,' she assured him.

'I was wondering if you wanted to go to youth group tonight. I'm dropping Joshua off in half an hour.' He smiled.

Sarah grimaced. 'I don't know anyone there.'

Dad gave an understanding look. 'I get why you feel it'll be awkward, but you really should go. It'll be good for you to make some friends.'

'Thanks for inviting me, Dad, but I don't want to go.' She gave him an apologetic smile.

'What if…'

Please just leave me alone.

'…you go in with Josh. I'll wait in the car for fifteen minutes, and if you don't like it by then, you can come home with me.'

Sarah rolled her eyes. *Ugh.* 'Fine.'

Dad grinned. 'Good. I'm sure it'll be great. You better get ready soon.' He walked out of the room.

Sarah sighed. 'Why did I agree to this?' she mumbled underneath her breath. She slid off the bed and walked to her wardrobe and went through her clothes to find her favourite pair of skinny blue jeans. She grabbed her black jumper and her light pink sneakers. She forced a brush through her tangled hair that hadn't been brushed for a few days now, then tied her thick, long hair into a high ponytail. Now all she needed was some make-up. Sarah grabbed her foundation powder and brushed it all over her face and neck. She picked out her mascara and thickened her lashes. Was the foundation covering all her acne?

Sarah looked down at her plain jumper. Too boring. She switched into a pink and navy hoodie, then looked in the mirror. That would have to do. Just as she was getting her bag, a knock sounded from the door.

'Who is it?'

'You ready to go?' her younger brother asked.

She shoved her phone into her bag. 'Yeah. I'm ready.' Sarah walked with her brother to the car, opened her door, and slid into a seat.

'See you later, Dad.' Joshua opened his door and shut it before Dad could reply, then ran over to join his friends at the basketball court.

Dad glanced over his shoulder in Sarah's direction. 'You going in?'

Sarah looked out the window. 'I don't want to go.' She slid down in her chair to show that she wasn't getting out.

'Come on, just give it a shot.'

She crossed her arms. 'No, I'm not going. Take me home.'

Sarah set up the projector in the Connect room, set out the chairs, and placed the snacks on the table. How far she'd come in just six months? She'd always been shy and had barely left the house. Out of fear of being rejected, she'd avoid talking to new people. But, with prayer, she'd grown in her faith and in confidence. She went to youth group and did make friends.

It all started when she'd seen that shy girl sitting by herself.

Sarah understood how uncomfortable the first time at youth group could be, so she stepped out of her comfort zone and walked across the room.

'Hi. I'm Sarah.' She held out a friendly hand.

The girl smiled up at her shyly and shook Sarah's hand lightly. 'I'm Annie.'

'Nice to meet you, Annie. So, is it your first time here?'

Annie's gaze flittered around the room. 'Um, yeah.'

'That's cool. Would you like to play basketball with me?' Sarah pointed to the doors to the basketball court.

Annie scuffed her cheap sneakers on the carpet. 'I'm not very good at it.'

'Don't say that.' Sarah tapped Annie's shoulder. 'I'm sure you'll be fine.'

'I doubt it.' Annie raised her head, but a sparkle was in her eyes. 'Okay, I'll give it a go…'

Loud voices interrupted Sarah's reminiscing as a few girls entered the Connect room.

'Hey, there!' Sarah hugged each girl. 'Come, have a seat.' She gestured to the semi-circle of chairs.

The scrapping of metal to the tiles filled the room along with giggly chatter.

'How's everyone been?' Sarah asked.

Each one replied with either 'Good' or 'Great'.

'Awesome,' Sarah clasped her hands. 'So, we'll start with a prayer, then get into this Bible study on the book of Esther.' Thankfulness filled her heart. 'Let's bow our heads and close our eyes.'

Selective listening
Anan Mclean

Selective listening is in the job description of childhood. In terms of fitting the job description, I would have been hired, paid and promoted to CEO on the spot. But on a dusty, orange afternoon, in a dirty town in northern China, I learned a valuable price for not listening.

Having missionary parents can be thrilling, but currently they were shopping — the most mundane activity a five-year-old child could endure. My younger brother, whose current entertainment level was in the negatives, asked to leave the shop. With my parents' permission, he left to play on a coin-fed, mechanical car outside. I, being a stubborn wanting-to-appear-mature child, didn't play with him. Not yet.

Infinity passed, and my parents were still browsing the shelves. The street did look nice. There was the paint-peeled mechanical car, rocking my brother back and forth. There was also a patch of trees, a very uncommon sight in China.

Never mind seeming mature, I thought. *I need to be out there.*

'Dad, can I play outside?'

'Alright, but just...' I had started walking.

'Did you hear me?' I stopped.

'Um, no.'

'I said, you must...'

I did try listening that time, but I still had no idea what he said. I was too preoccupied with the beckoning voice of the outside world. If I asked a third time, Dad might think I was being silly. Also, I was eager to play. I nodded, then left.

Finally free, I joined my brother on the car. It was much better than the shop, but soon I started to drift elsewhere. It wasn't every day we saw multiple trees in one spot. The mini cluster beckoned me.

'Hey, let's play over there!'

'But Dad said we're not meant to.'
'No, he didn't.'
'Yeah, he did.'
'He didn't say that to me!'

The argument went on a little longer. Being the elder brother, I won.

We trotted into the trees. For a while we just stood, touching the trunks and patting the branches. It wasn't every day we saw trees. Admiring trees was good, but only to a point. After all, we were boys; young, energetic boys.

We ran. We jumped around. Within seconds we were swinging from the branches. They creaked and groaned. Leaves were pulled from the treetops, snaps sounded from within the wooden limbs. We were ecstatic with freedom. Swinging joyfully on straining branches.

Nothing lasts forever. Our freedom soon came to a frightful end.

A man strode towards us, his face poisoned with fury.

The gardener!

His shouts were loud; spiteful words of Mandarin. We didn't understand him, but we knew he was furious. I wanted to tell him we were sorry. That we made a mistake and didn't know we were ruining his trees. But even if I had spoken, he wouldn't have understood. All I could do was stand, taking in his livid shouts.

I guess we couldn't blame him. How dare we hurt his trees! But presently, nothing but terror crossed our minds. The man seemed to get more and more agitated as he realised we couldn't understand him, let alone his language thick with fury.

We started backing away, but the man would have none of it. Shouting without let-up, he grabbed my brother's arm.

My brother's skin whitened in the gardener's iron grip, his eyes bulging with terror. This was one violent man. Realising he wouldn't let go, and that I was still free, I ran. I sprinted out of the

Selective listening

trees. I ran across the dust and into the shop, leaving my brother in the gardener's cruel hands.

I didn't know what to say, so I grabbed my dad and pulled him outside. My shaking hand pointed at the man, still roughly handling my brother.

There were many shouts in mandarin, and many angry gestures. But Dad stepped in and put his foot down. The gardener stopped yelling, and my brother was returned to Dad's side.

In the taxi-ride home, Dad gave us a well-deserved talking to.

'Why didn't you listen to me? I told you to *only* play on the car.'

'I didn't know!'

'But I *told* you.'

'I didn't hear you.'

My problem was obvious. I didn't hear him because I didn't listen.

'You should have asked me to repeat it.'

'But you already said it twice.'

'So?'

'So, you would've got annoyed.'

Dad paused. His face softened.

'No, I wouldn't. I would've wanted you safe. You should have asked me again.'

'As many times as I need?'

'Yes.'

I was relieved, but a little ashamed. I could have saved myself a lot of trouble if I had spoken out. But it was good to be safe. It was mercifully quiet as we drove on. I realised that I could ask for help, that I could indeed speak up. If I didn't understand something, I don't need to keep quiet. Dad only wants me safe.

As the taxi hummed onwards, I thought more about my dad. My father reminded me of something. It reminded me of many lessons fed into me since my earliest memories. Lessons saying that my God is the perfect father. Instructing, guiding, and loving me just as

Dad did through that turbulent afternoon. Breathing slow mist against the window, I decided to listen more closely to this other father in the future. I would let them both instruct me. They knew best. Relaxing further, I quietly watched through the dusty window and rested until home.

Lonely No More
Isaac Wong

Fear not, for I am with you: be not dismayed, for I am your God; I will strengthen you, I will help you, I will uphold you with my righteous right hand.
Isaiah 41:10

When I was young, I was very talkative and playful. Every time there was a Parent-Teacher Meeting, my teachers would complain about how noisy I was during class and say that I always caused distraction. When my parents heard this, they started to counsel me and threaten me by saying, 'If we hear your teacher complaining about you making too much noise in the class again, bad things will happen to you!' So I listened to them and tried to talk less in class.

As time went by, I started to become less talkative and instead grew extremely quiet. I was so quiet that I wouldn't even talk to my classmates and the people around me. Every day I went to school I would be that guy sitting alone with no friends at recess and lunch.

One day, a thought came to my mind telling me to start communicating more and mixing with the people around me, but I was too shy to be able to do that. Then I realised that the thought wasn't just an ordinary thought. It was God speaking to me. He was telling me to change. So, I prayed and asked God to help me to be able to communicate and mix with the people around me.

I waited for a week, and then another week, and still nothing happened.

One ordinary Sunday, I went to church and was talking to my friend, Victor, when suddenly a guy named Poh Ee came to us and invited us to the youth lounge. As I entered the room, I saw many new faces. Next thing I knew, I was sitting next to Victor listening to the conversation. Joel, one of the youths, came up to me and asked my name and how old I was. I was too shy to answer, so Poh Ee introduced me to him and the others.

As I slowly got to know them, I started to be able to communicate with people and I made many new friends from the youth group. I finally realised that God had answered my prayers. But I had another problem — how was I going to talk to the people in my school? Poh Ee wouldn't be there to introduce me! So I prayed. I prayed that God would give me faith to talk to people and make friends.

It was Monday and time to go talk and make friends with my classmates. I was afraid, afraid that they would judge me, afraid that I would be embarrassed in front of everyone. But when I introduced myself to one of my classmates, he was very friendly and nice to me. All of the things that I was afraid about were gone. I wasn't scared of talking anymore, and I started to talk to the people around me.

Now, every morning, every break, and at lunch time, I don't need to sit alone. I'm not lonely anymore. Thanks be to God!

The Fighter
Bastien Lee

I fought. I fought at school. I fought at home. I was the 'bully' to both my classmates and my siblings. I had a gang. I beat up my classmates. I got in trouble. I was called up. I was punished. And yet I fought.

As a missionary kid, I went to school in China, although one might have called it a 'farm'. We grew most of our food, we had animals, and many students spent time tending the school rather than studying. I was the 'foreigner' who could do whatever he wanted and ruled the classroom when the teacher was off. I kept my grades up, and so I stayed on the good side of the teachers. Back then, I would have called it 'thriving', I would have called myself 'cool', and would laugh as we smashed glass cups that we found into the girls' bathroom to 'scare' them. I would get into trouble. I would get sent to the principal's office and my parents were called frequently. They would take me home, disappointed in me once again.

It didn't stop there.

I fought my brother. These fights left us with cuts and bruises. We would lose control and give in to anger, frustration, and let loose until we did something that caused so much harm that we snapped back into reality, panic and regret flowing in our veins. We fought because we were the same. He was a bully, too. He was the dominant boss in his own class, and we were both too proud to step down.

My parents told me countless times that as the older brother, and as a Christian, I should set a much better example. But I didn't listen. Countless times my parents cried and prayed with me over the dining table because physical punishment proved useless. It seemed like I couldn't change, like I couldn't undo the personality that had plagued me for years. But every time my parents prayed for me, every time my mother sent out prayer requests to her friends, every time my parents sat with me, crying out to God to help me, begging him to act, to hear their prayers.

He heard.

He listened.

And he acted.

At the age of 11 I grew self-conscious. I saw that some of my friends truly liked me, but many of them didn't. That I was rather infamous for my actions. Against my expectations, those feelings against me never really changed, although looking back now, I suppose I deserved worse. It wasn't only the feeling of guilt and shame that drove me to change my actions, but the desire to be well-liked and respected.

Even after that I would still sometimes threaten and intimidate, but I was nothing like what I would have been if the Lord had not changed me.

I was in Grade 5 when my time in the local Chinese school came to an end. I was to change to an American-based international school. I left the 'farm' with some sorrow, but I looked forward to joining the American school.

I went to my new school with a handful of prayers behind me, prayers that were supporting me as well as hopeful pleas that I would no longer be a nuisance. And, once again, God proved faithful. On my first day, I was friendly. I was nice. I would even say I was popular, admired and respected. Not feared and despised.

I wonder now what would have become of me without the constant prayer to the Lord. I most likely wouldn't have joined the school that I attend now if it wasn't the faithfulness of my family and our Christian friends.

I am ashamed of many things that I did — many of the students I might have scarred emotionally, spiritually, and physically. Still, I am grateful for everything that was done for me in the years that I practiced physical violence. My transformation was not only a miracle, but also a testimony and a sign that God is faithful. It may

The Fighter

take him ten years, twenty, or even a lifetime to answer, but God hears us.
   He hears.
   He listens.
   And he acts.

He Answered

Sheann Tung

When Chermaine and I were younger, our family were always happy together and nothing ever got in our way. We were full of joy and peace. But one day, things started to change at home. Suddenly everything was about money. Our parents argued about not being able to afford to pay the bills and even thought that they couldn't feed their two beautiful daughters. From that time onwards, Chermaine and I were always crying in one corner of the living room. We would close our ears so that we won't hear anything. We were scared and didn't know what to do. We didn't know what was going on, either, and were just told, 'You are too young to understand!'

Why did this happen? Did I do something wrong? Why are they like this? How can I sort out this situation? Why won't anyone just help them?

Every time I tried to make things better by making funny jokes and doing silly dances to change the topic, it didn't work at all. Then I remembered how my Sunday School teacher would always tell us that if you prayed to God, God would definitely answer your prayers. At that time, I didn't believe in miracles because I'd tried it before. I'd prayed: *Dear Lord, I would like to have all the expensive things for Christmas... Amen.* But when Christmas came, I had only one gift. Even though I was grateful for the gift, I felt that God didn't answer prayers.

Sometime later, I started worrying about passing my exams to enter high school. I knew that if I didn't get a good grade, I wouldn't be accepted. So I started to study really hard each day. One day when I was studying, I started to cry, because all my fears were getting to me, so I pray to God for help. But without realising it, God was already helping me. He told my parents to send me to a Christian Learning Centre. This took the stress away about passing my exams.

He Answered

After a while at my new school, I noticed that things started to change. One day in school, I was marking my work when one of the supervisors came up to me and asked, 'Is everything okay?' Suddenly, I burst into tears, knowing my family was still struggling with problems. After an hour of talking about my situation at home and being prayed for, I felt much better, and I also felt God's assurance that he would guide me in this journey. I just knew that God told my supervisor to ask me if I was okay, so that all my anxieties and stress would be lessened.

Days went by and I could see that my parents were getting along much better and they were able to sort things out without arguing. I asked myself, *Did that prayer really work?* I was confused but at the same time I felt thankful that God had answered my prayers.

A while later, my parents had to pay my school fees. Knowing it would cost quite a lot of money, I decided to tell my parents: 'If you need help you should pray to God. He can help you through your difficult tasks if you pray to him.' They said they would take my advice and try to talk to God more seriously. A few days later, they were able to arrange the bills that they needed to pay. I realised then that God had helped me again.

A short time later I heard news that my parents believed God was helping them and they also said that their worries started to lessen, and I knew straight away he had helped again.

After all these years, praying and sharing my testimony has changed my life. I pray for others who are struggling with their own problems and tell them to ask God for help. I have spent so much time worrying in the past about so many things, and now the worry is gone! God helped me, and I know he will help others, too, if they put him first in their hearts and trust in him.

Surviving the Lockdown
Amelia Shee

Sometime in the year 2019, people started catching a dangerous disease called coronavirus or COVID-19. The symptoms include fever, cough, flu, and breathing difficulties. It may also cause loss of taste and smell. It is so serious that many people have actually died from this disease.

As COVID-19 became worse, the government of Malaysia declared a lockdown which is also known as MCO or Movement Control Order. During the MCO, everyone other than essential workers had to stay home to avoid spreading the virus. Many stores were closed including restaurants, cafés, and clothing stores. Furthermore, we were banned from gathering in large groups. Many people became jobless because they were not essential workers. People were also not allowed to leave their houses unless it was to buy groceries.

At first, I found it hard to adhere to the new rules, but with the help of God I was able to overcome it. Slowly, I adjusted to the new norm, yet there was another challenge I faced. The increasing cases and death rates caused me to feel fearful of what may happen next. I was also worried that people who are dear to me may catch the virus. Therefore, my family and I prayed that God would protect us, all our friends as well as relatives, from the virus. We also prayed for God to provide for all our needs, and the needs of the people around us. That we will have the essentials such as food, water, and a place to live. I asked God to heal the world and that the people who caught the virus will recover.

I am very blessed to still be able to attend classes and progress with my studies. This is because I attend a school called The Seed Resource Centre. In this particular school, we use the syllabus called the ACE program. We are allowed to read the text and study on our own. The supervisors or teachers will then mark our schoolwork once we send it to them via WhatsApp. Although my ballet exams were cancelled, I am incredibly grateful that I was able to continue taking classes via Zoom. I even had extra time to do things that I enjoy doing during the MCO. I had the opportunity to work on my talents. Moreover, I got a chance to renovate my room. Thus, at the end of MCO, I had cleaned, organized and decorated everything.

After about three months, the situation improved, and the government decided to lift the MCO. Many shops were allowed to open again, and people could start to travel within the country. Although there were less COVID-19 cases, people were still required to wear a mask and practice social distancing. Schools started to open and I managed to progress faster in my studies. God answered my prayers and provided for my needs. While many people had lost their jobs and are struggling to make ends meet, I thank God that we had the finances needed to buy essential items. God has been merciful to me.

Light Expels Darkness
Magda Alef

Over and over I kept asking myself: *What did I do wrong? Why are they treating me like this? What are they believing about me?* Then I fell on my knees, the tears flowed freely as I poured out my heart to the Lord.

'Please help me! Should I leave now? Should I run away, leave the country and never see these people again? Why didn't anyone speak up in my defense?'

I knew the Committee members had grown up together, and so there were things I would never understand. But they were all friendly and had always greeted me with a hug and kiss. I had been working with this group for over four years now; I thought they were my friends. Of course, I had accepted I was a white woman in a black community — different culture, different language, no connections. In a small town where everyone knows everyone, and almost everyone is related, I was never going to fit in completely. But after four years, I thought I might have been accepted.

What should I do? My first inclination was to run. I could just pack my bags and leave the country. I felt betrayed, lied about and totally vulnerable. After wrestling with my emotions for several hours, I fell onto the bed, exhausted.

I'd been invited by the Chairman to organise an international conference at short notice, as arrangements had stalled. The date was fixed by our international head office and attendance by senior officials confirmed. However, we were now facing a crisis — with just three weeks to go there was much to finalise.

The Chairman suggested I move into the flat above the office for the duration and in lieu of payment, I was not required to pay rent. This suited me perfectly. I relished the challenge and set to work. My previous experience organising conferences kicked in. I rang various supporters to join me in this mammoth task.

Light Expels Darkness

God's grace was evident as all the pieces came together. After endless calls, emails, and messenger chats, delegates representing nine countries confirmed their attendance. Representatives of all denominations responded with warm enthusiasm. I constantly liaised with the Chairman who gave encouragement and guidance. While it was a hectic preparation, I was pleased with the response.

At last the day came. The Chairman organized for the Worship team and myself to stay in a small hotel opposite the venue. This would enable an early setup, prayer and preparation before delegates arrived.

Ping! As I was setting out the chairs, an email arrived on my phone. Our opening speaker had been delayed by fog and missed his flight. Then two more speakers had flights delayed. I hastily re-organised the program. If there's one thing I've learnt in my years of conference planning, it's that things inevitably go wrong, so I needed to be flexible and unflappable. I was grateful that in the inevitable change of program, other international delegates willingly stepped forward to fill the gaps.

Despite all the challenges, the three-day conference, with around 70 participants, was a huge success. There were congratulations and heartfelt thanks from our parent organisation, including the President and International Director, who only made it for the last day. According to everyone, the aims of the conference were well achieved.

Immediately following the conference, in preparation for our executive review, I detailed all expenses, itemised reimbursements and reported on the organisational challenges and opportunities. I circulated these prior to the meeting.

All the Committee members arrived on time, but I sensed tension. Uncharacteristically, each person avoided greeting me. Instead of the usual handshake and hug, there was a quick glance in my direction and then they were greeting each other.

As minute-taker, needing power for my laptop, I was seated slightly back from the circle of Committee members. This was not unusual, and I tried to be at ease. The meeting was opened by the Chairman who prayed, thanking God for the successful conference.

As the meeting progressed I felt my heart begin to race. Member after member attacked various aspects of the organisation of the conference. They accused me of not consulting them, and not seeking approval of the whole Committee on various issues. They began to speak about me as if I were not there. I was not addressed, but unkind accusations were made without any opportunity for me to respond.

To make matters worse, a short time before the meeting I had been informed of a scandalous rumour that I was having an affair with the Chairman! I was horrified, as he was an honourable, highly regarded man, as well as a loving husband and father. I was old enough to be his mother and felt close to his wife, children and parents. Although we worked closely together, there was never any impropriety. These suggestions were devastating, but I was confident my friends would not entertain such rumours, especially as no-one had raised these allegations with me directly.

I could feel tears stinging my eyes. I was totally confused and my heart was aching. I debated whether I should run from the room, but I was jammed in the corner — and where could I run to? This was my home now.

As my report was analysed and debate raged about how they felt I had handled the finances, it seemed nobody could say a kind word about me. I was stunned and deeply hurt by their accusations. Not only were they surreptitiously accusing me of adultery, but now they were suggesting I had misappropriated funds from the ministry — the ministry I supported, heart and soul.

At last the meeting was over. After the Chairman's closing prayer, everyone pushed back their chairs and said goodnight, without acknowledging me. I was left in the empty room, all alone.

In the morning I decided to seek alternative accommodation as well as advice from the Chairman. I knew in my heart I had done nothing wrong.

On meeting the Chairman, I intended to be calm and matter of fact, but soon I was weeping and pouring out my heart. He listened sympathetically, encouraging me to keep things in perspective. The Committee members had known him since childhood — they were jealous of me. I was the foreign interloper who breezed in and took over. They resented my relationship with him. He urged me to take a deep breath, step back and trust in God for the outcome. He also assured me I had done a good job for which he was most grateful.

Over the next few weeks I avoided the Committee members and kept a low profile. While my first instinct was to run, my second was to just stay away from them. Slowly, the conviction began to grow that I must not to sweep this under the carpet but face it head on.

I began to think about the many missionaries and church leaders I knew who had suffered similar injustices which were not brought to the light. Deep scars resulted which sometimes did not heal. This resulted in immeasurable damage to their ministry and to them personally. I'd known people who had simply left with the issues unresolved. Some even lost their faith.

It did not take much research to find out who was behind the rumours. With a wildly beating heart I arranged to meet her for coffee. As we sat opposite each other, she agreed we should pray first. I asked God to help us both be honest, and to forgive us both for anything we had done wrong. Then I forced myself to look into her eyes and ask her directly, but gently, what evidence she had for her accusations. It soon became obvious that she was ashamed of what had happened.

With tears she sought my forgiveness. She said she was sorry — that it was a great misunderstanding. She confessed her jealousy and sought reconciliation. After everything was brought into the light, the air seemed sweeter. With much relief we cried and embraced one another.

Not long after, my season of service in that country unexpectedly came to an end, as the Lord clearly had other plans for me. At my farewell, those who had previously criticised me humbly thanked me. The Lord took me home and surrounded me with my children, grandchildren and loving friends. He assured me I was precious to him by renewing my sense of value and worth. He restored the years the locusts had eaten. He poured out his grace as he confirmed he is the Light of the World.

But if we walk in the light, as he is in the light,
we have fellowship with one another, and the blood of Jesus,
his Son, cleanses us from all sin.
1 John 1:7

An Angel in Heaven Now
Hazel Barker

'Our baby will be a boy and look like you,' I said, smoothing my dress over my stomach.

'Could be a girl who looks like you,' Colin said in a teasing tone.

From the very first moment we met, there had been a strong chemistry between us. Colin was so supportive of me. As the days passed, I grew to love him even more. I could not picture life without him.

In February of 1971, during the first few months of our marriage, I had been unable to find work as a teacher in Canberra, so I took a job as a kitchen maid in a hotel and scrubbed pots and pans. The worst chore was cleaning ovens. I choked over the grease and stink of kitchen waste and could barely keep myself from dry retching.

A few months later, I applied for a job in the Public Service and was accepted. Life was wonderful! We were so happy! I carried Colin's child, and my baby bump was growing month by month.

I was eight months pregnant in August, 1972, when I developed a loud, hacking cough. I would cough and spread my palms beneath my bump to protect our baby from the tremors that shook my body. Perhaps I knew, even then, that something was about to happen.

Each time I had a fit of coughing, a look of concern crossed Colin's face and fear vibrated within me like an alarm bell. The general practitioner prescribed penicillin tablets, and on our return home from the doctor, I took the first dose. Within minutes, I rushed to the bathroom and vomited. A sour smell rose. I rinsed my mouth and washed the mess down the sink. Colin rubbed my back and brought me a glass of water, then he raced to the phone and rang our doctor.

'Don't worry. I'll send a nurse around,' the doctor said in a matter-of-fact voice.

An hour crept by. A nurse came by and administered a needle. After she left, I broke out in a rash. My skin grew red and angry.

'It itches and burns.' My throat felt tight and my voice was high pitched. I collapsed on my bed.

Colin phoned our doctor and told him of my condition. He gazed at his wedding ring as he spoke, twisting it round and round his finger, waiting for a reply.

The doctor's urgent voice boomed over the phone: 'Admit her to hospital immediately!'

Within thirty minutes I lapsed into a minimally conscious state. I recall a nurse putting me to bed. There I lay, tossing from side to side, unable to distinguish between reality and nightmare. My sleep was disturbed by moans and groans. I vaguely recall Colin stroking my hair and speaking, drained of strength, as I lay helpless, unable to move my lips. My unconscious periods were interspersed by brief intervals of rationality.

One afternoon, somebody must have drawn the curtains because a shaft of sunlight pierced my eyes. A voice whispered, 'You've lost your baby.'

'My baby is born?' My voice sounded weak and hoarse.

'Well... you gave birth... but the baby's dead.'

My eyes, although open, could not distinguish anything but light and shadow. Like a cold steel blade, the words pierced my soul.

Impossible! Our baby couldn't have left us.

I checked my stomach — no longer firm and round, but soft and squishy. Nothing moved beneath my touch.

The baby I had nurtured within my body for eight months, is now no more.

Fear gripped me. Pain stabbed the back of my throat.

Is this a nightmare? Where are you, Colin? We have lost our baby! Did the little one look like you? We will never hear it laugh or cry or hold the precious bundle in our arms.

I soon collapsed into merciful unconsciousness...

In a haze of grief and medication, interrupted by doctors and specialists more interested in my vital signs than my state of mind, I remained in bed, too ill to go to our baby's funeral.

In numbed abstraction, Colin attended the burial. The sun spread its warmth that day, and feathery sprays of delicate green broke forth. The earth burst into life, but would forever hold our baby, still and silent, within its womb.

After the funeral, Colin entered my room. I recognised him for the first time and flung my arms around him. 'I haven't seen you for so long!'

'Been with you every day,' he assured me with a hug. 'I sent for your mother and met her at the airport... She's waiting outside.'

Mum entered. A look of unutterable suffering spread over her face as soon as she saw me. In her puffy eyes, red from lack of sleep, I read a reflection of my own grief.

Each morning, Colin would drop Mum off at the hospital, and she would sit beside me and pray. I drew comfort from my mother's presence but could not articulate my feelings of appreciation because I felt too weak to talk. My throat felt sore and it was painful to speak. Pain tore at my left side. Pain enveloped my chest with every breath. Pain wracked my entire body. I spent most of the day dozing, off and on.

After five more days in intensive care, the doctor removed the drip and I was shifted to another room. The illness reduced me to a mere skeleton, and I could only walk for a short distance to the toilet.

As soon as the doctor assured Mum the crisis was over, she returned to Perth. My heart ached for her. She had left me just when my health was improving and I could communicate with her without dozing off.

The days were long, and I yearned for the evenings, when Colin would visit me.

On the day I was discharged from hospital, sunlight streamed in through chinks in the blind. Birds sang outside my window. The hospital chaplain spoke words of comfort: 'Ask the Lord to heal your wounds. Pray for strength to bear the loss of your child. Remember that Mary lost her child too. She understands just how you feel.'

My mother had always instilled into me the love of Mary. I prayed and asked for strength. Both moral and physical. God's healing grace fell on me like snowflakes. I felt stronger. *Perhaps my health will return, and we'll be able to raise a family?*

Colin took me to the specialist's surgery to check on my progress.

Speaking slowly to emphasise the importance of his words, the specialist told me, 'You're lucky to be alive. Your liver was being consumed by your anti-bodies and the baby had a brain haemorrhage.'

Turning to Colin, he said, 'It may be too dangerous for your wife to conceive another child.' He hesitated before adding, 'Besides, she's not a young woman.'

Dark clouds enveloped me. *I'm in my mid-thirties, and Mum bore a child at the age of 48! Why can't we have another child?* I had thought my youthful dreams would be fulfilled when I found love, but now all my dreams were shattered. My joy extinguished.

For a brief period, it seemed as though the Lord had forsaken us. Still, I continued to pray for healing grace. I concentrated on getting strong again and took walks during the day. Colin accepted the tragedy with a stiff upper lip.

Months passed. August turned to October, and the skeleton trees burst into bud. The daffodils Colin had planted peeped out shyly to greet the warm sunshine. Slowly, my strength returned. We discussed the prospect of another pregnancy.

'Would Mary have suffered brain damage from the bleeding?' I asked.

'Perhaps...'

'She might have been like Herman,' I mused. My brother Herman had been born with infantile paralysis and couldn't talk or feed himself. He cried often — a piercing, heart-rending cry — and we never knew how to relieve his pain. Mary had been spared that much, at least.

Colin folded me in his arms. 'She's an angel in heaven now.' His voice sounded thick and hoarse. 'I'd rather have you than another child. I love you too much to risk losing you.'

When we visited Mary's grave, great sobs tore at my chest as I wept for the first time. Colin clasped me in his arms and joined his tears to mine. Our tears washed away our sorrow as we recalled God's promise in Psalm 34:8…

The Lord is near to the broken hearted and saves the crushed in spirit.

I felt as though a spring had been released within me. Our faith in the Lord pulled us through. His healing grace gave us the resilience to rise above our sorrow, and our love for each other would blossom over the next fifty years of fidelity. Fidelity to God's laws, and fidelity to each other.

My Piano Solo
Caleb Cheah

On a bright and sunny day, I thought to myself, 'It's going to be a good day today.' I had three tests to do in school that were urgent, and I told myself that accomplishing them was going to be a piece of cake. So I worked hard, and at the end of the day, I accomplished them all. The teacher gave me a form for a competition, which I took little notice of. When I arrived home, I did my homework while waiting for my parents to come home.

When my parents came back home, I passed them the form that my teacher gave me. My parents told me that it was an event selection form. When they asked me to choose which activities I would like to participate in, I decided to choose a piano solo and a few more other events. At first, I said to my parents, 'Don't worry, this will be easy for me.' But little did I know of the hardships I would go through.

A few weeks later in the evening, I was practicing for my piano solo. 'No! I keep getting this part wrong!' I cried out. 'I don't want to practice my piano anymore, it's too frustrating!'

'Son, you will keep on practicing!' my mom said.

'I can't, it's too difficult!' I complained.

A few minutes later, that same feeling of despair came over me. 'I don't know how to play this part! Why am I making this mistake again? This is just too difficult! I quit!'

Then, my dad asked me why I was so frustrated. I told him that it was because I did not know how to play the piano piece. My dad then helped me to understand the piece, and I continued to practice my piano. Finally, I was able to play the piece correctly.

A few days later, I came back home from school. I went to my room to change and then I started on my work. At that time, I suddenly remembered that I had a PowerPoint presentation to finish! 'Oh, no! I have a PowerPoint presentation tomorrow, and I need to revise my script! But… I have my homework to be done! What should I do?' I thought to myself.

Immediately, something my dad said to me popped into my head. 'Son, remember that when you don't know how to do something, always go to God and ask Him for help.' So I went to God in prayer and asked him to help me. For that day, I worked on my presentation and left my homework to do on the weekend.

The next day, I did my presentation successfully, but little did I know what was going to happen.

'Hi, son,' my dad said, when he got home from work. 'How was your presentation today?'

'Um… It went great!' I replied.

'Oh, yeah, you're supposed to do your science exhibit right?' my dad reminded me.

'Oh yeah, I am supposed to do that, but I have to practice my piano!' Then I started to feel frustrated again.

'Dad, could you give me a minute please?' I asked.

'Yeah, sure,' he answered.

So, I went into my room, I sat down on the bed, and I didn't know what to do next. Suddenly, a voice said to me, '…start praying…' So, I started praying and I asked God to help me.

'God, you know what I am going through, and you know that I am just frustrated with everything! Please help me to do all that I am supposed to do. So that through my work, I can glorify you. Amen!'

'Okay, Dad, can I practice my piano first, and then do the project? Because I have a whole bunch of stuff to do, and I can only do one thing at a time, so is that alright?' I asked my dad when I was done praying.

'Yeah, Son, I think that that would be fine with me,' my dad agreed.

So when I started to practice the piano, I didn't think of how badly I was playing the last time I practiced. Instead, I thought of how good I could become through God's help.

The day finally came when I would see how God has helped me so much. It was the day of my piano solo. When I saw the other competitors play, my heart sank, because they played very well.

When it was my turn to perform, the lady in charge of the event prayed for me. At that very moment, I could feel God take control and remind me that 'I can do all things through Christ who strengthens me' (Philippians 4:13). So with all the courage I had, I played the piano piece in a way I had never played before.

Finally, it was time to give out the awards. I was very surprised to find out that I had actually won 1st place! I was so amazed that I almost cried! 'God, thank you so much! You are just so good to me!' I said in my heart.

When I went back home, I thanked my parents for helping me with my project, and my piano piece, but most importantly, I thanked God, who all the while, was helping me to accomplish this piano piece to the glory of his name.

Invitation to Dance
Rhonda Pooley

September, 2019 in Battambang, Cambodia. It is the last night of the Chum Ben Festival — the night of the 'hungry ghosts'. The entire country is on the move during Chum Ben, with work and business suspended so that people may travel to their regions of origin. They go to the temples to appease deceased relatives who rise from the grave expecting sacrificial gifts of food and money. Great fear grips the nation, for the people dread the ghosts who appear to them during this time.

On the outskirts of Battambang, at the YWAM training centre, more than four hundred Christians — Cambodian nationals and NGOs (international workers from non-government organisations) — are gathering for an all-nighter of praise and intercession. I have flown in from Australia to attend the event, having been invited by my nephew, Gordon, who is one of the organisers. Stars begin to scatter across an indigo sky, and the chill night air is banished by flames from a huge brazier in the courtyard. Bicycles, cars and mini-buses pull in and the compound is soon filled with the sound of animated greetings in many dialects. Disposable cups of black tea are passed around, technicians test sound equipment, dancers shake out colourful flags. The excitement is in stark contrast to loud speakers blasting solemn Buddhist chants over the city.

A bracket of sound from ram's-horn shofars announces the beginning of the festival of praise. Backed by traditional instruments, modern guitars and keyboards, hands and voices are raised to celebrate Jesus Christ who has conquered death and hell.

Suddenly, in the middle of this soaring praise, my thoughts go to the opposite northern corner of Cambodia, to Ratanakiri Province, where Gordon is a church planter with Hill Tribe peoples. Seventeen years ago I was there, sitting in on a seminar for musicians and leaders from village churches. In the 1920s the first converts in the region had been told that traditional instruments were not acceptable for Christian worship. The introduction of western music, plus the widespread genocide practised by the Pol Pot regime, all but wiped out traditional music knowledge. However, Nye, a village pastor, remembers watching his grandfather making and playing traditional instruments, and today he is demonstrating the stringed instruments he has made from memory.

All the delegates at the seminar are eager to hear them played. Most are young people who have no experience or remembrance of such instruments, but they love the sounds they are hearing. They pluck at the strings and examine the undersides before passing them from hand to hand in awed silence. Body memory of lost culture comes to them through their fingers. There are tears.

At the close of that seminar I was invited to pray. I began by describing a vision that came to me in that moment. I saw a primitive hut, its door secured by an entirely superfluous padlock — a firm kick would shatter those flimsy slatted walls! Inside the hut, dusty and forgotten, were all manner of traditional musical instruments. I understood this to mean that the peoples' music had been illegally locked up. I knew God was saying to go in and take them back.

The next day, a Sunday, Gordon and I attended a house church meeting in Nye's home in Kun Chine village. As we climbed the steep ladder into the house, we came into a large, open room and saw that everyone was gathered around a 'stand' of eight gongs of graduating sizes. There weren't enough proper striking sticks to produce a sound from the brass discs, so rubber flip-flops ('thongs' in Australia) were being used as improvised 'dongers'.

'This is amazing!' said Gordon. In the moment I wasn't sure what he referred to, but I nodded enthusiastically because everything about this scene was wonderful to me; the open cook-fire on the slab of stone in the middle of the room; the rich aromas of what turned out to be lunch; the colourful woven mats on the floor; the graceful wrap-around skirts worn by both men and women. Over lunch, Gordon told me it was the use of the gongs that amazed him. He explained that early converts were told the gongs belonged to Buddhism and so, for love of Jesus Christ, the people had renounced them, even though the very sound of them resonated with their innermost beings. It was their heart-sound.

Later, I learned that these particular gongs had been borrowed from Nye's brother, the village headman, who rejected the Gospel because he viewed it as the missionaries' religion and had no relevance to his culture. Nye had asked to borrow them after the interpretation of the vision. That afternoon, non-believing villagers gathered at the foot of the ladder to listen to Christians worshipping Jesus with the gongs. Afterwards, several came to faith and joined the group in Nye's stilt house.

In the ensuing seventeen years, many have learnt to use the gongs, and other traditional instruments, to accompany Christian worship. And now, at this Night of Praise in Battambang, I see the gong players taking a strategic role in exalting the name of Jesus Christ over a land that is gripped by fear of death. By 3 am most of the intercessors and musicians are taking a rest, but the gong-players, traditional drummers, and a small group of twenty intercessors continue to press through the oppressive atmosphere of Chum Ben.

Gordon whispers to me to dance. 'Dance? I can't dance!' I say, thinking he means the graceful movements of Khmer dancers. I am appalled by my mental picture of this overweight septuagenarian daring to attempt anything so elegant. 'No,' laughs Gordon, seeing the look on my face. 'War dance!' And understanding dawns. This is to be a prophetic act of spiritual warfare against the powers of darkness. I move closer to the gongs and take up a warlike stance. I begin to dance — my version of something resembling a Mâori Haka or a native American Brave stomping the ground! One by one, other intercessors join in and now gong players and dancers work off each other, co-ordinating sound and movement. Voices rise in worship-warfare. It is the final push to victory in the unseen, spiritual realms.

Just before dawn, the dancing changes from warfare to triumph. It is as though Moses has lowered his staff and Miriam has taken up the tambourines at the crossing of the Red Sea. A great and noisy shouting breaks out as the other intercessors and musicians return to join the triumphant celebration.

In the brazier only embers remain, but the sky is tinged with many shades of orange and pink. In the spirit life of Cambodia, a new dawn is rising.

My Asthma Story
Moses Yong

It was night when I awoke to the sound of people talking. I looked around me and saw a full moon shining outside the window. Then I heard someone talking again. I turned around and saw a man whom I recognised as my family's doctor. He was talking to my mum. They kept on talking, and I didn't have anything to do. So I tried to go back to sleep.

After a few minutes, I still could not fall asleep. Then I heard a voice and realised it was the doctor speaking. I heard these dreadful and terrifying words, 'Your son has asthma and he won't be able to eat ice cream and run around from now on.'

I thought to myself, 'Oh no! I can't eat ice cream anymore.'

I looked through the window and thought about what the doctor had said. I kept wondering why I could not eat ice cream. Then I remembered that there was a time when I went to the hospital. I had been eating ice cream but then started coughing. I felt very uncomfortable, so I cried. I told my mum I was coughing, and that my throat hurt, and she had sent me to the hospital. That was the first time that I heard that I had a disease.

Asthma is a condition in which your airways narrow and swell. This makes breathing extremely difficult. The symptoms of asthma are wheezing, coughing, and shortness of breath. I found out that these symptoms will appear when I do the things the doctor told me not to do.

The next morning, I went to the park with my mum. An ice cream truck went by. I looked at it, and looked at my mum, hoping that she would buy me an ice cream. I asked her, 'May I have some ice cream?' She paused, and thought hard about how to respond to my question. Instead she held my hand, and we continued walking. She did not reply my question.

So as a child I wasn't able to eat ice cream and run around like other children. I felt that God was unfair. I said to myself, 'Why does God treat me so badly?'

But then I started praying every day that God would heal me. I would sit on my bed and say, 'Dear God, thank you for this day. Thank you for dying on the cross for me. Please heal me from my asthma. I would like to run around and be able to eat ice cream again. In Jesus' name I pray. Amen.'

Every month other church members would also pray for me. I would stand in the center of a group of people and they would lay hands on me. I felt touched that they would take the time to pray for me.

Years passed and my asthma was getting better and better.

When I turned twelve, God healed my asthma and I was fully recovered. I was very happy that after all the perseverance, I can finally eat ice cream. I learned to trust in God and to never give up.

Misunderstood
Val Russell

As a young girl with Autism, I waited patiently in the immigration queue, unaware that my life was going to change forever. They said we were going to Australia, but I didn't know anything about Australia. I didn't really understand the significance of moving, nor how that would change my life forever. I tried to shut out the noise. Babies were crying, mothers and fathers yelling. Then a much louder noise, as the speaker blared out the next call. Was it our turn? My sister was crying again but I knew better than to complain or tell her to shut up like I normally would, if I was confined inside the walls of my English home. Instead, silent tears stung the corners of my eyes as they always did when my sister cried.

Terror gripped me. I wanted to run home, to familiarity. Inside it felt like my heart was jiggling up and down and all the blood from my head was draining down into my heart, overfilling it, making it pump faster and faster. Make it go away. I must make it go away. I tried my hardest until I literally felt nothing. Like a robot, I just obeyed. I followed my dad as close as possible and walked onto the plane. I sat in the seat and did up my seat belt. They gave us cards to play with and a pin of the aeroplane.

Taking off was awesome! I loved being high in the sky.

Both my sisters cried all the way on the first leg of our journey into a foreign country. Thankfully, we were allowed to disembark for a short time while the plane was being refuelled. All I wanted was to feel safe on solid ground and be able to move around. Standing to my feet, I looked out the window. There were men with brown skin everywhere, rifles in their hands ready to be used at any moment. I shivered. 'Where are we?' I asked.

'Bahrain,' my mother replied. I didn't recognise the name, wasn't even sure I heard it right. Mum looked scared. I looked at my dad. He had the best poker face you have ever seen. Whatever he was feeling or thinking, I could not tell. Was he feeling unsettled like me? Maybe he was missing his family. The threatening guns below us stood their ground, alert and ready to fire. I wondered why. In my ignorance, I wondered why they needed guns. I had no idea. It was 1970 and my mum said this was a dangerous place. What she really meant was, we were in a conflict zone.

I wished I could have held my dad's hand. I wished he had known how I felt, but he didn't. I may as well have been invisible. My dear dad, did he not understand how much I loved him? Did he not know how much I needed his reassurance, his love? I watched as my younger sister, the cute toddler, tried to run ahead. Dad grinned. Normally he would have laughed at her, but not today. Clearly, he was worried about something. My little sister was lucky because they understood her.

Before returning to the plane, my mum went to the toilet. She told us there was only a hole in the ground. Disgusting! I decided not to go to the toilet in this weird place.

With a sudden jolt, the plane slowly reversed out of the terminal. Finally, we were getting out of this war zone that I never wanted to revisit. I wondered if the people that lived there were nice or did they all carry guns to frighten off visitors?

As we flew on top of the clouds, panic threatened to overwhelm me. I pushed it down as far as it would go. I didn't want to be called a 'cry baby' again. My mum would always say to people, 'Oh don't worry about her, she cries when anyone else cries.' No, I must not cry. Misunderstood, autistic ten-year old girls shouldn't cry. I put the lid on my panic. This is an adventure, I told myself, a new life in a new place, I must remember that. A new land, new soil.

I was so high in the sky and I realised I don't belong anywhere right now. Neither where I came from nor where I was going. That was enough to make a little girl panic. I will belong though, in the new land, I told myself. This time I will make friends, good friends that want to be with me. It's all about being a good girl, friendly and polite. It will be better this time; I know it will. It just means I have to try harder.

'To be something you're not?'

'That's not true you know. Everyone can be a friend!' I responded to my imaginary friend. He was always picking me up on things. I'm going to prove him wrong this time.

'But you don't know the first thing about friendship.'

'What do you mean? Of course, I do. I just have to be nice. That's what my mum says.'

'People drive you mad. They drain you of energy. You don't really want to be their friend. You just want to be someone special.'

'Maybe you should go for a walk now. You've said enough.'

I watched my imaginary friend grin and walk away. Once more I became aware of the droning of the plane as it zoomed through the sky. I couldn't stand sitting in one place for so long I really had to move. Be a good girl I told myself, while inside I was in total panic. Trying so hard to hold it together, a tear slipped from one eye. Will I ever see my cousins again? It's an awful long way to this new land. Will I ever see my Grandma and Grandpa again? What about my aunties and uncles? I will miss my Aunty Iris; she is really nice.

I already missed the garden and my bike. They were my getaway places, especially when I knew I was in trouble. What will it be like in the new land? Will I have a garden? Will there be a place for me to hide? The sky was so blue up here. I could imagine me sitting on the wing, the sun making me shine like a star — wishful thinking? The wind blew my hair and it froze on the spot making me look like some crazy bloke in some funny cartoon. Smiling to myself I adjusted my pillow. The motion of the plane made me sleepy and another tear of panic slid down my cheek.

Oh, what's happening? I jolted awake and realised the plane was bumping around everywhere. Nausea gripped me as I became aware of my fear. My sisters were both crying. The older of the two looked like she would vomit any minute. She probably would. She always does. I was glad I was two seats away from her. Then suddenly, the journey became smooth again.

My stomach lurched again as I felt the plane drop. We were in the middle of the clouds; the sun was gone. I asked Dad what was happening, and he said we were descending. I presumed that meant we were going down. I didn't want to ask, because I knew he thought I was stupid. As we closed in on the earth below, I saw houses, but not as many as where we came from. There were hills or were they mountains, I'm not really sure. The sky was such a beautiful rich blue and my heart warmed at the sight.

My uncle was going to be meeting us. I was looking forward to seeing him again; he had been away from us in this new land for a long time. As we stepped out of the plane into the tunnel, a warmth hit us. Kind of like walking into a warming oven. New smells overwhelm me as they always do. What *is* that smell?

We moved from place to place, moving slowly through long queues. So many people coming to Adelaide. Dad handed over the passports and sighed when he heard them being stamped. Finally, we were through and looking for our luggage. Staring at the suitcases. We didn't have much. Everything was left behind; in the only place I ever knew. My sisters and I each had a small tea crate of our treasures that would come later. Mum and Dad were given one big crate each. Our entire world was in those tea chests. We had shrunk, considerably.

Carrying our meagre bags and cases, we moved through the doors into the new land. It took my breath away. There stood my uncle and aunty and their two little boys. I was so overwhelmed, I had nothing to say. A traumatic twenty-four hours was finally over. Little did I know that the adventure, had only just begun.

Andy
Craig Chapman

It had been an unusually mild week in New York City. Above average temperatures and clear skies yielded no rain, let alone the 'White Christmas' we had craved.

The upside was that we were able to explore the crowded streets of Manhattan in relative comfort. On our last night before departing for a New Year stay in Hawaii, I wore my coat more out of habit than necessity. The biting cold of Boston, our previous stopover, was still influencing my choice of attire.

Yet it wasn't hard to imagine the wind funnelling between skyscrapers and snow being furiously scraped, shovelled and ploughed from streets and pavements. No doubt this would soon be the case. I thought about the inevitability of a change in the weather, when my thick, padded coat with generous hood and thigh-length hem might have been invaluable.

My family and I picked our way through the masses toward the restaurant we had chosen for dinner. I noticed a smattering of homeless people, strung out and sitting with their backs against a walled section between shopfronts, meagre possessions all within reach. One man in particular caught my eye. I quickly looked away, refocussing on our destination. He appeared to be adequately dressed for the conditions. I tried not to think about what he would do when the cold came.

That guy could really use your coat…

Was it just a guilt trip? Or was it something more… a prompting, perhaps? I kept walking initially, but then faltered. We were just outside the restaurant when I made the decision.

'Go in without me,' I said to my wife. 'I'll be back in a few minutes.'

I retraced the few hundred meters to where I had passed him. Approaching awkwardly, I knelt on the pavement in front of him.

'Do you need a coat?' I asked softly.

It was some time before he realised he had been spoken to. It seemed he was not accustomed to conversing with others to pass time on the streets.

He looked up at me, slowly. 'Everything helps,' he said with a shrug and a hint of a smile.

I spoke with him for a couple of minutes, carefully probing for some sparse details about his circumstances. I peeled off my coat and gave it to him. He nodded approvingly.

'Nice coat!' he offered, in thanks.

I explained that it had come from Australia. I hoped it would serve him well. My awkwardness returned as I stood to leave. Clearly, I would never see Andy again.

I returned to the restaurant. My wife looked at me as I sat down.

'You've lost your coat,' she smiled.

I smiled back, contentedly.

In my experience, God is not in the habit of making demands on us. But he persists with gentle promptings. We do well to pay attention.

Another Happy Memoir

Baxter Gierus-Heintze

I love hospital and nursing home meals.

Now, I know what you are thinking. He's gone mad. He's such a spud. But don't worry; it's fine. The question is: Why do I love these meals?

Before my dear Gran and Grandma went to heaven in 2016, my family (Mum, Grandma, my sister Ella, and me) were visiting Gran at Estia Homes while Dad was at the Australian Lutheran College studying to get ordained as a pastor.

We were at Estia for the entire day, which meant that we had to have lunch there. And a cup of 2-minute noodles wouldn't cut it. I mean, I did like 2-minute noodles, but I would've probably still been hungry. I eat like a machine. So we sat outside at a table, as it was pretty sunny, and we had what was on the menu: lamb chops and gravy with mashed potato and cooked vegetables.

It was about time I tried lamb. Dad kept chirping on that, 'Lamb is delicious,' and, 'You should try lamb, Baxter, it's amazing!' This was my opportunity to try it!

After we said grace, I took a bite.

Then I asked, 'Is anyone not hungry?' IT WAS DELICIOUS! One of the best bites I ever had. Thanks be to God that Gran and Grandma were there. Thanks be to God that I got that opportunity!

Pretty soon, everyone ended up giving me all their lunch. That meant that I ate four meals in one sitting!

'Ach, dear me!' is what my German-speaking Papa said when I told him about it back at home.

After lunch, we went back to Gran's room. We had a little devotion, and I read a Bible passage to Gran. At the end, Gran said what she always said, 'Go with Jesus.'

Go with Jesus, I wondered. I could tell that Jesus was present. At the meal. At the little devotion. Jesus is always with us.

Gran was 95. All of us thought she would make 100 and get a letter from the Queen.

And Grandma was 72 then. We all thought she was energetic and healthy, and wouldn't go anytime soon.

Fast-forward four years, however, and all is not well. Two years without Grandma and Gran. Two years without their wisdom, influence, and care. Today I still grieve.

Also, school hadn't been going how I would've liked it to. I like to get lots of As, to be the smartest, but I found myself getting a B every now and then and even Cs occasionally (I have high standards). I was fatigued. Not only that, I felt alone. Alone, without Grandma's shoulder to lean on, alone without Gran's wise words, without proper guidance. I did have my parents. And Papa. But things weren't the same. I felt like a little fish stranded in an ocean.

I felt that I was not the same person that I was the previous year. I felt that Jesus had left me.

But something made me change that opinion.

It was cold, the 4th of June, and it was a bit after midday. I had just finished my piano lesson when I realised that I actually had Music class! So I rushed off to Music, arriving at 12.25. The lesson started at 12.05, So I missed all of what the teacher was explaining.

I asked, 'What on earth are we doing today?'

He said to me, 'Baxter, do you have your trombone?'

'Yes.'

'Alright, you're up.'

I didn't know what he was talking about, but then he mentioned solos! I had to play a trombone solo in front of the entire class, which I did not expect!

By now, I had turned pale, and the butterflies roared like V8s in my stomach. Since Grandma and Gran had gone, my confidence had taken a drastic landslide.

Another Happy Memoir

So, as I got my instrument out of the storage room, I prayed. I prayed, hoping that God hadn't abandoned me. I prayed that Jesus would still be with me, be that shoulder to lean on, like Grandma, be willing to share wisdom, like Gran.

Then, I picked up my trombone, and made my way to the front.
'So, what will you be playing for us today?' asked the teacher.
"Advance Australia Fair…"
'I heard you play this one before.'
'…and 'Click Go the Shears."
Then I played.

Although I had prayed, there were still challenges, primarily to concentrate, to just look at my music. But it turned out well. I thought it was not good enough, but everyone seemed to think it was pretty good.

I couldn't have done that. Not in the state that I was. That was Jesus with me. That was the support of Grandma and Gran, living on in Heaven.

I got through it well and ended up getting an A.

But that was the least of my thoughts.

I finally had my confidence back. I didn't need lamb to remember Grandma and Gran. I needed Jesus. I needed him to be with me. And he was, is, and will be forever.

We were saying a prayer with Gran, just before we were to leave. After we said 'Amen,' she said to all of us, 'Go with Jesus.'

Suitcases

Elizabeth Turland

My time in Egypt was my life. The people there, my family. The culture. My culture. Everything I had ever known. I remember once, during our home assignment, driving into my grandparents' driveway and asking, 'Where are we?' At the time, I didn't know that in another couple of years, I would be driving into this driveway again, this time, knowing we might never go back home. My friends, my family. I didn't know that in the next years, all I would have of Egypt would be the suitcases in which we carried our belongings back to Australia. All I would have would be the suitcases. The suitcases that were full of memories, the complete opposite of my heart, which was empty and hurting.

The driveway that I had been so excited to drive into when I was a child, three years before this dreadful moment, would stay with me. But that was a child's mentality. A child that didn't know the hurt that it would be facing. That driveway. The driveway to dread. The dread that I felt, knowing that if I ever did go back to Egypt, not all my friends would be there. Most of them would be gone. And the people that were left we would only see for a week or two. The hurt I was feeling was indescribable. I kept asking my parents, 'When are we going home?' but they just kept telling me that this was my home now.

But it wasn't. 'Australia Is Not My Home.' That's what I kept telling them, but they wouldn't listen. They just kept telling me, 'You'll get used to it,' and, 'Please just stop,' and, 'You know that it is your home.' They wouldn't listen.

Egypt was my home. I would never fit in here. I spoke Arabic and could put my hair into a hijab. I didn't know the latest songs, or that it was 'uncool' to read books and like homework. I had no idea who Brittany Spears or Hugh Jackman were. But I could tell you random facts about Egypt and explain the ideals of a Muslim. I didn't fit in.

Suitcases

A few weeks after we got back we moved from my Grandma and Grandpa's house to my Nanna and Grandad's house. There, I met my puppy that would become my best friend, with whom I could share all my troubles and memories without fear of being judged. The suitcases were brought out again and again to my puppy. His name was Pharaoh, just to fill up another suitcase. Pharaoh was the end of one suitcase, and the start of another. Pharaoh was the connection to Egypt that I needed in Australia. He was the courage to keep going and the companion to ease the pain. He was the suitcase that helped me through every hard time.

When I had to go to my new school, I went through the suitcases, carefully examining every memory. From the time I taught my friend English, to filling up the suitcases to go on holiday, to finally the last suitcase, and packing away all our belongings in the bags to take to the airport, and giving away all the belongings that we didn't need to the Africans that worked at Dad's school, African Hope Learning Centre. I filled up many suitcases of memories from that school: going to the houses of the staff, eating their traditional food, the soap competition.

The suitcases made me cry. I didn't want to go to a school where I knew I would be judged for not knowing the culture of Australia. I wanted to go back to my school, where everyone knew each other and were friends. Mum and Dad brought in the final suitcase memory. Pharaoh. Dad brought him in and put him in my bed for the night, even though he wasn't allowed inside. This gave me the courage to go to school and just be me. The suitcase was full. The memories were stuffed so hard in the suitcases that they were beginning to break. The suitcases that I knew and had given me so much happiness, were breaking.

After I came home from school that first day, I found that my suitcases were gone. My parents had thrown them out. I was distraught. All my memories were in those suitcases. I ran into my room and threw myself down on the bed. Why had they done that?

They knew that those suitcases were my only connection to my Egypt friends. And that connection was gone.

But my parents came into my room solemnly holding all the memories that I thought I'd lost. I lifted up my head and saw the memories. The ones I thought were gone. But the thing that I learnt was that my parents cared. They had carefully taken all the memories out and saved them for me. The suitcases were just holding the memories. My parents and I put my memories into new suitcases. It wasn't the same, but we laughed and cried over the memories. Yes, I never thought that I would fit in here, but now I have friends that will laugh and cry over things with me.

Leaving Egypt didn't mean cutting off the connections I had with my best friends. They still are my best friends, we just have to put more time into being friends. It's more work, but it's worth it. I know that I am loved. And now, here in Australia, I can start filling up more suitcases with the many memories I have and will continue to make.

Isn't it time you told your story?

This year, 51 people have had their stories published, and nine of them have been recognised as category winners. Do you have a story of faith and testimony? Will 2021 be the year you tell your story?

For the possibility of being published or winning a prize, please send us your true stories in one of these three categories:

Eternity Matters Short Stories of Life
(up to 500 words)

Immortalise Young Stories of Life
(500 – 1000 words for writers aged 17 and under)

Tabor Stories of Life
(1000 – 1500 words)

Submission details, rules and writing resources can be found on our website:
https://storiesoflife.net

Have you written a book?
Not sure how to get it published?
Worried it will cost a fortune?

Not a problem.

Helping writers to become authors

info@immortalise.com.au
www.immortalise.com.au

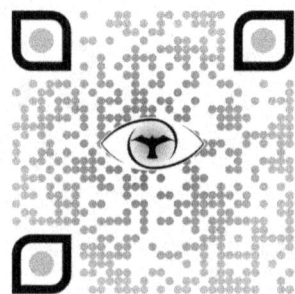

www.ingramcontent.com/pod-product-compliance
Lightning Source LLC
Chambersburg PA
CBHW070255010526
44107CB00056B/2472